THE
ORIGIN OF
SIN

Decoding the Nephilim Legacy
in Our Genetic Code

PRP, DR. BENJAMIN MARTINEZ

FIRST EDITION

This book is dedicated to my wife, the one person who's always believed in me and the plans and purposes of God for my life, Pastor Josie Jalil Martinez.

"And I will put enmity between thee and the woman, and between thy seed and her seed, it shall bruise thy head, and thou shalt bruise his heel," (Genesis 3:15 KJV).

ENDORSEMENT FOR
ORIGIN OF SIN

"Origin of Sin" by PRP, Dr. Benjamin Martinez is a captivating exploration into the theological origins of sin, masterfully weaving together biblical narrative and scholarly insight. From the very first page, Martinez grabs readers' attention with a gripping hook, leading them on a profound journey through the depths of creation and the complexities of sin's inception. With meticulous attention to detail, Martinez delves into the biblical accounts of creation, sin, and the role of angels, deftly drawing upon scripture to support his thought-provoking theories. Each chapter unfolds like a tapestry of revelation, unraveling the mysteries of biblical prophecy and theological interpretation. From the intriguing proposition of a pre-Adamic creation to the profound implications of Lucifer's rebellion, Martinez challenges readers to reconsider long-held beliefs and embrace a deeper understanding of God's redemptive plan. "Origin of Sin" is not just a book—it's a scholarly odyssey that will inspire, enlighten, and forever change the way you view the Bible and it's timeless truths.

Pastor Dr. Jacqueline Nieves-DeLaPaz-Casa
De La Paz Ministries (An English Speaking Virtual Ministry)

TABLE OF CONTENTS

ACKNOWLEDGMENTS

I want to thank my Lord and Savior, **Jesus Christ,** for always being there for me, dying for my sins, and allowing me to live my life for Him. I want to thank the **Holy Spirit** for never leaving me as I went through all the testing grounds in this journey. For placing great men that were apostles, prophets, teachers, and pastors ahead of their time in my life to give me the foundational tools that inspired me to become a student of the Word, an apostolic and prophetic teacher, and now an author. From the Earth's foundations, You chose me to accomplish Your perfect will upon the face of the earth.

To my best friend and **loving wife,** thank you because you never stop believing in me. We have been through some difficult times in our 42 years of marriage because of my poor choices, but you always stood by my side, even when you had the legal right to leave and start a new life.

I thank God that you came into my life at the age of 14 years old; you're a fabulous woman of God whom I'm still so much in love with, and I'm honored to be able to call you my wife as we take on the challenges of this new chapter and journey of our lives.

To my spiritual father, **Apostle Danny Bonilla,** I still remember the day I walked into your office. I was a New York City Police Officer, going through a very difficult time in my life. When I walked into your office, you began to share with me how you had received a prophetic word about a police officer that would come to your office asking for help in the previous weeks.

In 2020, you lost your life to COVID-19, but I want to honor you for being a great example of a man that truly loved God and thank you for sharing your life with me. The prophets told you that I was your Jonathan, and we would have a relationship like Jonathan and David in the Bible.

You took me on as a spiritual son, and we spent countless hours studying the Bible; I got to travel with you and obtained exposure to the apostolic and prophetic ministries in the late 80s.

To my parents, **Maximino Martinez**, AKA Freddy El Ex Brujo, and **Carmen Rodriguez**, I know you divorced when I was very young and I was raised without a father, but I want to honor you both. Mom, thanks for introducing me to the fear of the Lord and giving me the godly principles I have today. And my new dad **Crescencion Rodriguez,** thank you for taking care of my mom and loving my siblings and me unconditionally.

Raising four children on your own in Harlem, N.Y. was very difficult, but you did a fantastic job because we are all serving God and have done well in our academia and chosen professions; you're a tremendous woman. Dad, you were never really in my life, and I don't know how you ended up marrying my mom since your family was involved in witchcraft and you were a satanic high priest, but the Bible does declare to beware of wolves in sheep's clothing.

You finally had an encounter with God and renounced your covenant with Satan. I can't say much about our relationship because we never really had one, but thank you for being the instrument God used to bring me into this world. Two years before you passed away, I heard the voice of the Lord, loud and clear, telling me that I needed to get on a plane and fly to Puerto Rico and make peace with you, and I'm glad that I did.

To my best friend and brother, **Prophet Brad Kimberly**, from the day I met you in Duluth, Minnesota, God joined our hearts as we spent countless hours praying, studying, and teaching the Word of God.

You always had a word in season for me, and when I found myself in discouraging times, when it was hard to trust in what God had spoken over my life, you were always there to encourage me. I don't understand why God took you home so early, but I love you, and I know you're in heaven cheering me on to finish the race. Thank you for allowing your daughter, Rachel, and your grandchildren into my life; they are incredible.

To **my in-laws** who lost their lives to Covid-19 in 2021, I want to thank you so much for loving me as your son. I genuinely consider you both as Armor-Bearers in my life. I have chosen to give you the title of Armor-Bearers because even though you were both close to your 90s, and it seemed like your daughter and I were taking care of you, you were taking care of us.

You both were my spiritual bodyguards, protecting me in prayer, wisdom, and counsel so that no harm would come to me as I studied God's Word and drove clients to supplement my income until I walked into that which God has spoken over my life. Thank you for all the wonderful years you gave me, and most of all, thank you for the amazing wife I love so much.

To my siblings and their spouses, **Rachel Riley, Ruth Diaz, Daniel Martinez,** and **Chistine Peña,** thank you for all the support you have given me through the years. I am so proud of the men and women you have become. Continue to leave a mark as God uses you as prophets, teachers, and pastors in His Kingdom. And to my other siblings through marriage and their spouses, **Jimmy Jalil, Janet O'Toole,** and **Juan Jalil,** I love you guys so much, and I want to thank you for all the support that you have given Josie and me throughout the years; thank you for always encouraging me to write and believing in me.

This book would not be possible without the support of my sister, **Ruth Diaz,** who's supported me through some of the most difficult times in my life.

In Memory of:

Apostle–Danny Bonilla

Prophet–Brad Kimberly

Armor–Bearer Alfredo Jalil

Armor–Bearer Ascuion Jalil

Police Officer–Lauren Kresse Jalil

Prophet–Danny Ramos

Deaconess–Beatrice "Candy" Gandia

INTRODUCTION

I expect as you take a journey through the pages of this book that you will become intrigued with the Biblical worldview of creation and the narrative of humanity as we race towards the last days for a God that is working out His redemptive plan for the human race. I pray the readers will discover a book that is more than a story about giants, angels, demons, and a pre-Adamic world, but the reality of a real spiritual war between two seeds and the seed of the serpent that is trying to annihilate the human race.

After reading this book, I hope at least one person is able to change their paradigm and worldview about aliens, UFOs, transhumance, artificial intelligence or angel intelligence, and discover the truth behind what some would call alien technology. (I believe there is Biblical evidence that this is angel technology.)

This book is an instrument for promoting Biblical creation that acquaints us with Adam, the first human given charge to care for and protect the Garden. Adam was given the authority in a place where he would commune with the Lord Himself and His manifested presence (Genesis 2:7-9).

In an age where there is so much propaganda about Christianity, Islam, LGTBQ, BLM, and the philosophies of man, people no longer know what camp they belong to and have rejected the one true God who created the first human in the Garden inside Eden, which was the original temple where God and Adam would walk together.

Adam was the priest that God ordained over the Garden and the earth. God also established the institution of marriage in the Garden between a man and a woman. This might be difficult for many to accept, even within the church, and may contradict your worldview or paradigm, but the reality is that if you're a Christian, you're a "creationist."

"And the Lord God caused a deep sleep to fall upon Adam, and he slept; and He took one of his ribs, and closed up the flesh in its place. Then the rib which the Lord God had taken from man He made into a woman, and He brought her to the man" (Genesis 2:21-22 NKJV).

There are so many strange ideas concerning the origin of sin and creation that have blinded many. Even Christians are men walking in bondage between truth and error. But according to the Genesis account, the woman is not named Eve until after sin; even though they lived at least 4,000 years before they sinned, sin still existed on the earth; this is why God said, "The man has now become like one of us, knowing good and evil. He must not be allowed to reach his hand and also take from the tree of life and eat, and live forever," (Genesis 3:22 NIV).

The Bible also tells us that there was a day when Lucifer sinned: "How art thou fallen from heaven, O Lucifer, son of the morning! How art thou cut down to the ground, which didst weaken the nations! For thou hast said in thine heart, I will ascend into heaven. I will exalt my throne above the stars of God: I will sit also upon the mount of the congregation, in the sides of the north: I will ascend above the heights of the clouds; I will be like the most High. Yet thou shalt be brought down to hell, to the side of the pit.

They that see thee shall narrowly look upon thee, and consider thee, saying, Is this the man that made the earth to tremble, that did shake kingdoms; That made the world as a wilderness, and destroyed the cities thereof; that opened not the house of his prisoners?" (Isaiah 14:12-17 KJV).

After Adam and Eve sinned in the Garden of Eden, God made a prophetic declaration that would echo for generations to come and declared war and judgment on Satan and his seed. God, in His infinite wisdom, "Declaring the end from the beginning, And from ancient times things which have not been done, Saying, 'My purpose will be established, And I will accomplish all My Good pleasure'" (Isaiah 46:10 NASB).

Throughout the history of the church, traditionally, the church and theologians have always ascribed that the origin of sin came through the first man, Adam, "but the from the tree of the knowledge of good and evil you shall not eat…" (Genesis 2:17 NIV).

According to Scripture, I want to declare to you that if we apply the basic principles of hermeneutics, which is "the theory and methodology, especially in the interpretation of Biblical texts," [1] then as students of the Word of God, when rightly dividing the Word of God, we should allow Scripture to interpret Scripture. If we are going to rightly divide the Word of God, sin did not originate with Adam, but according to Scripture, sin originated with Lucifer.

In Ezekiel 28:11-19, there was a prophetic declaration that the prophet Ezekiel was making, and he was speaking of a time when the King of Tyre, or his original name, Lucifer, was cast out of heaven before kings and in the sight of all who were watching among the nations because sin was found in him. So according to Scripture, sin originated with Lucifer.

This Nephilim theme involves the origin of sin; an overview of creation; the seed of the woman and the seed of the serpent; the Nephilim, a new species that altered the genetic disposition of God's creation; Satan's plan to corrupt the birth of the seed of the woman, the Messiah; as it was in the days of Noah, and afterward, giants appeared again after the flood.

The framework of understanding the components in the redemptive history is investigated and presented in Scripture through this theme as a storyline, as a hematology theme, which shall be consummated in Lucifer, his bloodline, and fallen angels awaiting eternal judgment, as well as an angelic invasion that will fulfill Biblical prophecy in the last days.

Matthew, the author of the First Gospel, a tax collector who accepted his role as one of the Apostles after accepting Jesus Christ as his savior, declares in Matthew 24:37-39 (KJV), "But as the days of Noah were, so shall also the coming of the Son of Man be. For as in the days before the flood, they were eating and drinking, marrying, and giving in marriage. Until the day that Noah entered the ark, and knew not until the flood came, and took them all away; so shall the coming of the Son of Man be." God's plan for His redemption has unfolded across history despite the progressive manipulation of Satan upon God's creation.

1

THE APPROACH
OF THIS BOOK

As we investigate and summarize God's unfolding theme of the Bible storyline, the Theme is God's plan of creation, and the origin of sin, from a creative perspective.[1] The next effort, as an organizing principle, is to relate the Biblical events of creation to the theme of hamartiology in the landscape of the existence of humanity and the supernatural world of the Watchers, "Angels." We will discover Biblical teachings and archeological findings on the subject that will take you through a journey of 6,000 years of Biblical history and this present day.

"We will begin with the theological presupposition that Scripture constitutes a developing story under one unified theme that reveals and interprets God's redemptive acts that develop across time, from creation to new creation, and His redemptive plan with His chosen people.

God plans to redeem His fallen creation to the Father through Christ, and God Himself reveals this plan progressively through history, employing His redemptive plan. Throughout His Word, He does this ultimately so that He's glorified."[2]

I want to look at Biblical theology, which is the study of the Bible from the perspective of creations. What can we learn about this particular theme for this specific era of creation and about the next era of creation and redemption as God unfolds this particular theme and revelation as the human race progresses towards the end of a 6,000-year period of redemption?

The term "progressive" does not imply the "progressive covenantal." This book is based on the Reformed tradition with the doctrines of Sola Scriptura. Sola Scriptura is a theological doctrine held by most evangelicals and Protestant Christians in their denominations that the Scriptures are an infallible source of authority in the Christian faith and practice ("Scripture interprets Scripture") and are the final authority of Christian doctrine.[3]

As we look at the Scriptures' perspective of creation, the Bible gives us an account that there was a day God asked Job, "Where were you when I laid the earth's foundation? Tell me if you understand. Who marked off its dimensions? Surely you know! Who stretched a measuring line across it? On what were its footings set, or who laid its cornerstone, while the morning stars sang together and the angels shouted for joy?" (Job 38:4-7 NIV). God is declaring to Job the events of Genesis 1:1: In the beginning, God created the heavens and the earth as He spoke the earth's foundations into existence. I want to declare to you the Bible never puts a time stamp on the events of Genesis 1:1.

The Bible declares there was a time when God and Lucifer sang together with the morning stars, and the angels of heaven would shout for joy. The morning stars are a specific group of angels, and I believe the Scriptures make it clear that the morning stars and a group of angels would lead all of creation into worship. So the question is, if they were leading the earth into worship, who were they leading as the angels would shout for joy? As we continue to build on the theme of creation and unfold this narrative through the Biblical lens of creation, we will discover that a pre-Adamic creation existed.

Before Adam or a pre-Adamic creation existed, God created spiritual creatures and sentient beings called *seraphim*. Each had six wings: with two wings they covered their faces, with two they covered their feet, and with two they were flying (Isaiah 6:2-3 NIV).

"Cherubim's, and I knew that they were the cherubims. Everyone had four faces apiece, and every one had four wings, and the likeness of a man's hands was under their wings. And the likeness of their faces was the same, which I saw by the river of Chebar, their appearances and themselves: they went every one straightforward" (Ezekiel 10:20-22 KJV).

Archangels, the word *archangel*, has its origins from the Greek word *arkhangelos*, meaning "chief" in Hebrew. Archangels are high-ranking angels such as Michael, Raphael, Gabriel, Uriel, Sariel, Raguel, and Remiel; they are given the title *sarim*, meaning "princes," to show their rank and status in the Bible.

Thrones, the Bible through Ethan the Ezrahite the songwriter of the tribe of Levi, the son of Zerah, is able to give us some insight of the hierarchy of these angles who ranked third within these angels who are on God's council are the first two rankings of angels the Seraphim and the Cherubim, these angels meet directly with God to handle the affairs of all creation (Psalms 89:7; Daniel 7:9 KJV).

Dominions, these angels are known for carrying out God's will, they are also messengers and managers of God. A great example of these angels is found in the Bible in the book Genesis. In this narrative, Dominions Angels appear to Lot at the city gates, and all the men of the the city of Sodom surrounded Lots house for they wanted to have sex with these angels but they were struck with blindness and could not find the door. These angels came down to warn Lot and his family to get out of the city because the Lord was about to destroy the city. So the angels instructed them to flee for their lives and not to look back, but his wife disregards the angel's warning and turned into a pillar of salt (Genesis 19: 1-15).

Powers, the Bible also tells us these angels are also known as angels of authority. They are known for assisting humanity over satanic assignments, witchcraft, evil forces, demons, and the demonic forces waging war against the children of God. These angels are warriors, soldiers, and ready to defend the Church at the command of the Holy Spirit. "He will command His angels concerning you to guard you in all your ways" (Psalms 91:11; Hebrews 1:4; Psalms 91:11-12; Hebrews 1:13 ESV).

Principalities, these angels have been given the assignment to govern over the political and religious affairs of the world, they are assigned to global politicians, government, military, cities, states, towns, institutions, and the Church, and they govern with a scepter. "So that the manifold wisdom of God might now be made known through the church to the principalities and authorities in the heavens" (Ephesians 3:10, 1:21; Colosssians 1:16, 2:20 NASB).

Virtues, these angels poetic in their mechanism with the ability to control the elements such as storms, thunder, rain, lighting, and earthquakes, but also are known for miracles and assisting humanity in their faith in God" (Exodus 19; Matthew 24: 29-30).[4]

In the book of Daniel, it says, "The prince of the kingdom of Persia withstood me twenty-one days, but Michael, one of the chief princes, came to help me, for I was left there with the kings of Persia," (verse 10:13 ESV). And Jude 1:9 (ESV) says, "But when the archangel Michael, contending with the devil, was disputing about the body of Moses, he did not presume to pronounce a blasphemous judgment, but said, 'The Lord rebuke you.'"

In the ineffable tapestry of creation, there exists an order of beings. Angels are high-ranking beings who have been visiting planet Earth since God spoke the world into existence; sometimes, when they appear on the earth, they will seem like the male species and are usually tall. This order of beings eludes the scope of our scientific paradigm and rational thought. "And there came two angels to Sodom at even, and Lot sat in the gate of Sodom: and Lot seeing them rose up to meet them, and he bowed himself with his face forward to the ground, and they performed judgment on Sodom and Gomorrah" (Genesis 19:1-5 KJB).

The Apostle Paul in the book of Hebrews says, "Keep on loving one another as brothers and sisters. Do not forget to show hospitality to strangers, for by doing so some people have shown hospitality to angels without knowing it," (Hebrews 13:1-2 NIV). Angels, celestial beings, Sentient beings, or the Ancient Race have been visiting Earth from the beginning of time and at times can shapeshift into the image of a human.

The prophetic book of Revelation mentions that there will be more angelic activity in the last days as angels are mentioned most in this book, as the events of the end time unfold, and creation witnesses these angelic beings protecting and declaring judgment on the earth. The angels are also seen sealing the foreheads of the servants of God, Michael and his angel fighting against demonic forces, another angel binding Satan for a thousand years, and we also see them guarding the gates of the New Jerusalem. The existence of these sentient beings has been pivotal from the beginning of time in the fabric of creation and the events of the last days (Revelation 1-12).

The book of Genesis states that God created the heavens and the earth (Genesis 1:1 KJV). I want to declare the origin of sin did not start with Adam and Eve. It started with Lucifer as he went in and out of the earth, teaching creation and the people that inhabited the earth billions of years before Adam and Eve were created, and by "By the multitude of thine iniquities, in the unrighteousness of thy traffic, thou hast profaned thy sanctuaries," (Ezekiel 28:18 ERV).

I have always been fascinated with the Bible and the concept of creation, angels, demons, the natural world, the spiritual realm, and human history within this paradigm. As we study the personality of God, we will, through history, see He has always created with a purpose. He created the earth so that man would be fruitful and multiply. He did not make the world formless and void, but something happened, and the earth became a wasteland as the Spirit of God hovered upon the face of the deep (Genesis 1:2 BSB).

In the following chapters of Genesis, we see God is creating a new heaven and earth (Genesis 1:3-31). Thus, it's preeminently the history of creation. The Bible reveals that the creation or creations of this earth's reality developed throughout the Bible in human history. Regardless if this does or does not fit your paradigm, we must focus on the theological presupposition that Scripture constitutes a developing story under one unified theme that reveals and interprets God's redemptive acts that develop across time, from creation to new creation, and His redemptive plan with His chosen people.

2

THE ORIGIN OF SIN

The Bible reveals that the creation or creations of this Earth's reality developed throughout the history of the Bible. Biblical archaeologists have discovered and confirmed many of these events throughout the past century, and the Biblical views on creation and the scientific fact of the archaeology state that the age of the Earth is about 4.5 billion years old and 65 billion years for the universe. Many theologians and Christians believe the Earth is about 6,000 years old.

"Christian physicists have examined the age of the Earth and have discussed reasons for the controversy over this issue and how these can be resolved. They also drew from several fields of science, ranging from the Earth's geology to cosmology, to show that the scientific evidence clearly favors an age of 4.6 billion years for the Earth and about 14 to 65 billion years for the universe." [1]

Many Bible believers and theologians believe that God's creation of the Earth and the "days of creation" in Genesis 1 occurred at once. These believers are known as "young Earth creationists."

Most believers believe what science has found through modern technology and geological findings are false because they believe the Earth was created 6,000 years ago. If we look at Scripture in Genesis 1:1, it states, "In the beginning, God created the heavens and the earth."

God has never put a time stamp on the time of the creation of the Earth. Then something occurs in verse 2 of Genesis 1, which states, "And the earth was without form, and void: and darkness was upon the face of the deep."

Notice that it states, "the earth was without form and void." To better understand this verse, we must look at the original Hebrew interpretation. The word void in Hebrew (*tohu* and *bohu*) does not mean that the Earth was not finished but that it was in a state of total desolation.

According to *Webster's Dictionary*, the word *desolation* is synonymous with *devastation*. So now, if we examine the word *destruction*, according to *Webster's Dictionary*, it means "desolation, ruin, havoc, loss, depredation, demolition, or waste." So what caused the Earth to become a wasteland in Genesis 1:2?

To validate that God did not create the Earth in a void state, we must look at what Isaiah, the prophet, said about the Earth. Isaiah 45:18 states, "For thus saith the Lord that created the heavens; God himself that formed the Earth and made it; he created it not in vain, he formed it to be inhabited: I am the Lord, and there is none else." God is particular that He did not create the Earth in vain (void) or in chaos. Now we must look at the word "was" in Genesis 1:2.

In the Hebrew language, the word "was," when translated, is "became," so if we read Genesis 1:2 properly, it would read like this: "Now the earth *became* desolate and empty, darkness was over the surface of the deep, and the Spirit of God was hovering over the waters."

The book of Jeremiah, one of the major prophets of the Bible, uses the same language as Genesis 1:2. Jeremiah states, "For my people is foolish, they have not known me; they are Sottish children, and they have none understanding: they are wise to do evil, but to do good they have no knowledge. I beheld the Earth, and, lo, it was without form, and void: and the heavens, and they had no light. I beheld the mountains, and, lo, they trembled, and all the hills moved lightly. I beheld, and, lo, there was no man,

THE ORIGIN OF SIN

and all the birds of the heavens were fled. I beheld and the fruitful place was a wilderness, and the cities thereof were broken down at the presence of the Lord, and his fierce anger. For thus had the Lord said, The whole land shall be desolated; yet I will not make a full end. For this shall the earth mourn, and the heavens above be black; because I have spoken it, I have purposed it, and I will not repent, neither will I turn back from it," (Jeremiah 4: 22-28 KJV).

If we are going to use proper hermeneutics and allow Scripture to interpret Scripture, then it's clear that Jeremiah was referring to Genesis 1:2 when he states "the earth was void and formless." [2]

In the book of Isaiah, Isaiah gives us a prophetic declaration and a look into the past as he declares, "How art thou fallen from Heaven, O Lucifer, son of the morning! How art thou cut down to the ground, which didst weaken the nations!" (Isaiah 14:12 KJV). Job was able to shed some light on a past event that tells us that Lucifer was cast into the earth and weakened the nations. Scripture is telling us through the prophet Isaiah that when Lucifer was cast out of heaven into the earth, the earth was populated. This might be difficult for some Christians to accept because it does not fit their paradigm or Biblical theology, but we must follow the storyline of creation as the events of creation unfold.

This proverb of Solomon states, "It is the glory of God to conceal a matter and the glory of kings to search out a matter" (Proverbs 25:2 NET). There is no such thing as a new revelation. Still, as you can see, God has declared through King Solomon that He has concealed the truth for a season, and it's for our glory to search out the Scriptures; God has hidden many truths throughout the Bible for His church. As we approach the Biblical narrative as we are living in the last days we shall see that what was concealed in previous generations will be revealed to the Kings of the end time church.

Continuing to search out the Scripture to validate that sin did not originate with Adam and Eve, but with Lucifer, the storyline progressively expands under the repeating theme of '(re) creation, the fall, and redemption,' a cycle that repeats itself until the seed of the woman crushes the seed of the serpent (Genesis 1-3). Willem VanGemeren thus notes, "Creation, in a real sense, is the preamble to the history of redemption."

Furthermore, history will not end until God's sovereign; the outset shows that creation's 'beginnings' were initiated with a future goal intended, an eschatological purpose. Thus, the prophets and the apostles could speak of the end in terms of the beginnings, new heavens and new Earth (Isaiah 65:17; Revelation 21:1). As we continue to follow this narrative, we shall see the Holy City, the new Jerusalem, coming down from God, prepared as a bride beautifully dressed for her husband (Revelation 21:2).[3]

Moses is able, through prophetic interpretation and his prophetic writings, to give us the accounts of creation in Genesis 1:2 of a sovereign God speaking light into existence after the destruction of an earth that was formless and void because of Lucifer. The Apostle John is able to shed some light on God's description in the book of Revelation of a more glorious creation where God and the Lamb are the temple, there is a New Jerusalem for all the nations of the earth, and there is an organic, redemptive plan for humanity. Willem VanGemeren says, "The Bible begins with the account of creation (Genesis 1-2 NIV) and ends with a description of a more glorious creation (Revelation 21-22 NIV)."

This is why the prophet Ezekiel begins with giving an account of creation, where the progressive plan of God for redemption in judging Lucifer and the world in Genesis 1:1 is revealed. This world existed in the expansion of time where, in the beginning, God created the heavens and the earth to be inhabited by His creation, for there were kings, kingdoms, nations, and people until Lucifer corrupted them by trafficking iniquity. As a result, God judges the earth, so His progressive plan to redeem the earth is executed.

Moreover the word of the Lord came to me, saying, "Son of man, take up a lamentation for the king of Tyre, and say to him, 'Thus says the Lord God: "You were the seal of perfection, Full of wisdom and perfect in beauty. You were in Eden, the garden of God; Every precious stone was your covering: The sardius, topaz, and diamond, beryl, onyx, and jasper, sapphire, turquoise, and emerald with gold. The workmanship of your timbrels and pipes was prepared for you on the day you were created. You were the anointed cherub who covers; I established you; You were on the holy mountain of God; You walked back and forth in the midst of fiery stones. You were perfect in your ways from the day you were created, till iniquity was found in you.

"By the abundance of your trading you became filled with violence within, And you sinned; Therefore I cast you as a profane thing out of the mountain of God; And I destroyed you, O covering cherub, From the midst of the fiery stones." Your heart was lifted up because of your beauty; You corrupted your wisdom for the sake of your splendor; I cast you to the ground, I laid you before kings, that they might gaze at you.

"You defiled your sanctuaries by the multitude of your iniquities, By the iniquity of your trading; Therefore I brought fire from your midst; It devoured you, And I turned you to ashes upon the earth in the sight of all who saw you. All who knew you among the peoples are astonished at you; You have become a horror, And shall be no more forever" (Ezekiel 28:11-19 NKJV).

In this narrative of Ezekiel 28:11-19, the prophet of God tells us Lucifer, by the abundance of his trading, became filled with violence within, and he sinned; another word for trading is trafficking. In the book of Colossians, we find the same language—the Colossians and Lucifer were trafficking the stability of the Gospel for false teachings. These false teachings were a result of a mixture of culture, philosophies, and religious ideas that were threatening the Gospel. I believe Lucifer was also replacing the order of government God had ordained as he functioned as high priest over the earth. The Bible tells us that the last days shall be like the days of Noah; once again, in the twenty-first century, Lucifer has corrupted God's creation to worship Him by instituting the philosophies of man and a mixture of religious and cultural ideas, just as in the beginning and in the time of the Colossians (Colossians 1:13-29).

"The redemptive-historical approach of the storyline builds on the theme by emphasizing the rule of God on earth and the interrelation of man and his Creator. Lucifer, the high priest of the earth, is entrusted with the stewardship of God's creation; God is betrayed and must assert that He is God and that there is no other. In His anger, He destroys the first Earth with water and fire in Genesis 1:1." [4]

And in His anger, in order to continue with His redemptive plan, He reveals to King David the events of Genesis 1:1. In a prophetic moment, He takes King David to a place where he's having a vision of a different time.

"Then the Earth shook and trembled; the foundations also of the hills moved and were shaken, because he was wroth. There went up a smoke out of his nostrils, and fire out of his mouth devoured: coals were kindled by it. He bowed the heavens also, and darkness was under his feet. And he rode upon a cherub, and did fly: yea, he did fly upon the wings of the wind. He made darkness his secret place; his pavilion round about him was dark waters and thick clouds of the skies.

At the brightness that was before him his thick clouds passed, hailstones and coals of fire. The Lord also thundered in the heavens, and the Highest gave his voice; hailstones and coals of fire. Yea, he sent out his arrows, and scattered them; and he shot out lightnings, and discomfited them. Then the channels of water were seen, and the foundation of the world were discovered at thy rebuke, O Lord, at the blast of thy nostrils" (Psalms 18:7-14 KJV).

What an incredible prophetic moment! As God stirred His prophets in the past, He's also stirring His prophets today during a time when there is so much darkness. Those Five-Fold ministers who move in the prophetic, and especially those called to the office of a prophet, you know there are times when God will take you to someone's past through a vision and allow you to see what they have experienced, much like what King David experienced concerning the events of Genesis 1:1. This type of prophet is called the seer prophet that moves through visions and dreams, and this peculiar prophet's emphasis is on two spheres of this anointing, according to *Strong's Concordance* (H7200), *ra'ah*, to see, to see perceive, to see, have vision, and *Strong's Concordance* (H2372), *chozeh*, a beholder of vision, to look upon with approval, agreement, prophet, see that, seer receiving insight and prophetic revelation.

God is speaking to His creation and to this generation today through dreams and visions, and He also spoke to His creation in the past in the same manner, for in the book of Hebrews, He declares, "Jesus Christ the same yesterday, and today and forever" (Hebrews 13:8 KJV). God is guiding this generation like He did with past generations by speaking to His people through prophets and through ordinary people through the gift of prophecy or the spirit of prophecy, or through those who hold the office of a prophet to overcome the many challenges we face in this generation.

Prophets and the prophetic gift will give the church guidance and an edge in a time when this generation will experience the pages of the Bible come to life as the church races toward the end time prophecies.

The Septuagint, which is the oldest extant form of the Old Testament, the version most quoted by Jesus and the disciples, and the only translation from the Paleo-Hebrew alphabet, used in Old Testament times, provides more clarity on Lucifer. Ezekiel 28:13-19 describes him adorned with nine different jewels, which were all worn on his breastplate. If we take a look at the High Priest of the temple in ancient Israel, as with Genesis, early Jewish traditions name Moses the author of the book of Exodus.

Applying the basic principle and pattern that Scripture interprets Scripture within the field of hermeneutics, the book of Ezekiel gives us evidence that Lucifer was the high priest of a pre-Adamic world that existed in Genesis 1:1, which the Bible never puts a time period on, but we know it existed before Adam and Eve were created.

In Exodus 28:9-29 KJV, Moses gives us evidence of the priestly attire worn by Lucifer as the high priest of the earth:

And thou shalt take two onyx stones, and grave on them the names of the children of Israel: Six of their names on one stone, and the other six names of the rest on the other stone, according to their birth.

With the work of an engraver in stone, like the engravings of a signet, shalt thou engrave the two stones with the names of the children of Israel: thou shalt make them to be set in ouches of gold. And thou shalt put the two stones upon the shoulders of the ephod for stones of memorial unto the children of Israel: and Aaron shall bear their names before the Lord upon his two shoulders for a memorial. And thou shalt make ouches of gold;

And two chains of pure gold at the ends; of wreathen work shalt thou make them, and fasten the wreathen chains to the ouches. And thou shalt make the breastplate of judgment with cunning work; after the work of the ephod thou shalt make it; of gold, of blue, and of purple, and of scarlet, and of fine twined linen, shalt thou make it. Foursquare it shall be being doubled; a span shall be the length thereof, and a span shall be the breadth thereof.

And thou shalt set in it settings of stones, even four rows of stones: the first row shall be a sardius, a topaz, and a carbuncle: this shall be the first row. And the second row shall be an emerald, a sapphire, and a diamond. And the third row a ligure, an agate, and an amethyst.

And the fourth row a beryl, and an onyx, and jasper: they shall be set in gold in their enclosure. And the stones shall be with the names of the children of Israel, twelve, according to their names, like the engravings of a signet; every one with his name shall they be according to the twelve tribes. And thou shalt make upon the breastplate chains at the ends of wreathen work of pure gold.

And thou shalt make upon the breastplate two rings of gold, and shalt put the two rings on the two ends of the breastplate.

And thou shalt put the two-wreathen chains of gold in the two rings, which are on the ends of the breastplate.

And the other two ends of the two wreathen chains thou shalt fasten in the two ouches, and put them on the shoulder pieces of the ephod before it.

And thou shalt make two rings of gold, and thou shalt put them upon the two ends of the breastplate in the border thereof, which is in the side of the ephod inward.

And two other rings of gold thou shalt make, and shalt put them on the two sides of the ephod underneath, toward the forepart thereof, over against the other coupling thereof, above the curious girdle of the ephod. And they shall bind the breastplate by the rings thereof unto the rings of the ephod with a lace of blue, that it may be above the curious girdle of the ephod, and that the breastplate be not loosed from the ephod. And Aaron shall bear the names of the children of Israel in the breastplate of judgment upon his heart, when he goeth in unto the holy place, for a memorial before the Lord continually.

These garments are not your ordinary garments, but a holy God designed holy garments separated for the high priest to bring honor and glory to God, as they would lead the people of God to the presence of God as worshipers.

The Scriptures give us more than enough evidence that Lucifer was the high priest in a pre-Adamic world; following his rebelling, he was removed from his authority over the earth and cast down to the earth. Because of his rebellion, God destroyed the first creation with fire and water, and the whole Earth was totally submerged in water, not flooded like in Noah's flood. And this is why King David declares in the Psalms, "He made darkness his secret place, his pavilion round about him were dark waters and thick clouds of the skies," (Psalm 18:11). Darkness was upon the face of the deep, and the rainstorm is the tent where Jehovah makes His secret place until He decides to call forth the earth from the water. This is why Job also declares, "Who can understand how he spreads the clouds, how he thunders from His pavilion?" (Job 36:29 NIV).

In the narrative in Genesis 1:2, we can observe that King David and Job are using the same language, and once again, applying the basic principle and pattern that Scripture interprets Scripture, within the field of hermeneutics. Throughout all the Scriptures, there is a river that flows and declares with a loud voice that God did not create the world in chaos or void, and this is why Isaiah clearly states, "For thus says the Lord, Who created the heavens, Who is God, Who formed the earth and made it, Who has established it, Who did not create it in vain, Who formed it to be inhabited: 'I am the Lord, and there is no other" (Isaiah 45:18 NKJV).

3

OVERVIEW OF CREATION

"The Scripture presents a developing narrative with a clear pattern from the beginning to the end: the kingdom of God is an eschatological concept, connecting creation with the new creation. It is eschatological since it has been inaugurated with the creation and will culminate as united in the end." This is why Paul the Apostle declares, "That in the dispensation of the fullness of time He might gather together all things in (Christ) both which are in heaven and which are on earth—in Him" (Ephesians 1:10).[1]

"Then I saw a new heaven and a new earth, for the first heaven and the first earth had passed away, and the sea was no more. And I saw the holy city, New Jerusalem, coming down out of heaven from God, prepared as a bride adorned for her husband. And I heard a loud voice from the throne saying, 'Behold, the dwelling place of God is with man. He will dwell with them, and they will be his people, and God himself will be with them as their God. And he who was seated on the throne said, 'Behold, I am making all things new'" (Revelation 21:1-3 ESV).

"In the beginning" means inauguration, but it also anticipates the end. Scripture presents with the beginning, the end, and the connecting meta-story. The story is that God, the Creator, has hidden the days of redemption in the days of creation."[2]

Many theologians in the past and in the present day have been in conflict about the second coming of Christ; the reason for this is that they have not followed the basic principles of interpreting Scripture. This is why it is so important to understand creation because in the days of creation are hidden the days of redemption, connecting this eschatological theme.

The answer to this question concerning the days of creation and the days of redemption are found in the Bible, and we must begin with creation "in the beginning" in Genesis 1:3-31.

And God said, Let there be light: and there was light. And God saw the light, that it was good: and God divided the light from the darkness. And God called the light Day, and the darkness he called Night. And the evening and the morning were the first Day. And God said, Let there be a firmament in the midst of the waters, and let it divide the waters from the waters.

And God made the firmament, and divided the waters, which were under the firmament from the waters, which were above the firmament: and it was so.

And God called the firmament Heaven. And the evening and the morning were the second Day. And God said, Let the waters under the heaven be gathered together unto one place, and let the dry land appear: and it was so. And God called the dry land Earth; and the gathering together of the waters He called Seas: and God saw that it was good. And God said, Let the earth bring forth grass, the herb yielding seed, and the fruit tree yielding fruit after his kind, whose seed is in itself, upon the earth: and it was so. And the earth brought forth grass, and herb yielding seed after his kind, and the tree yielding fruit, whose seed was in itself, after his kind: and God saw that it was good. And the evening and the morning were the third Day. And God said, Let there be lights in the firmament of the heaven to divide the Day from the night; and let them be for signs, and for seasons, and for days, and years: And let them be for lights in the firmament of the heaven to give light upon the earth: and it was so. And God made two great lights; the greater light to rule the Day, and the lesser light to rule the night: he made the stars also. And God set them in the firmament of the heaven to give light upon the earth,

And to rule over the Day and over the night, and to divide the light from the darkness: and God saw that it was good. And the evening and the morning were the fourth Day. And God said; Let the waters bring forth abundantly the moving creature that hath life, and fowl that may fly above the earth in the open firmament of heaven. And God created great whales, and every living creature that moveth, which the waters brought forth abundantly, after their kind, and every winged fowl after his kind: and God saw that it was good. And God blessed them, saying, Be fruitful, and multiply, and fill the waters in the seas, and let fowl multiply in the earth. And the evening and the morning were the fifth Day. And God said, Let the earth bring forth the living creature after his kind, cattle, and creeping thing, and beast of the earth after his kind: and it was so. And God made the beast of the earth after his kind, and cattle after their kind, and every thing that creepeth upon the earth after his kind: and God saw that it was good. And God said, Let us make man in our image, after our likeness: and let them have dominion over the fish of the sea, and over the fowl of the air, and over the cattle, and over all the earth, and over every creeping thing that creepeth upon the earth.

So God created man in his own image, in the image of God he created them; male and female he created them. And God blessed them, and God said unto them, Be fruitful, and multiply, and replenish the earth, and subdue it: and have dominion over the fish of the sea, and over the fowl of the air, and over every living thing that moveth upon the earth. And God said, Behold, I have given you every herb bearing seed, which is upon the face of all the earth, and every tree, in the which is the fruit of a tree yielding seed; to you it shall be for meat.

And to every beast of the earth, and to every fowl of the air, and to every thing that creepeth upon the earth, wherein there is life, I have given every green herb for meat: and it was so. And God saw everything that he had made, and, behold, it was very good. And the evening and the morning were the sixth Day. Thus the heavens and the earth were finished, and all the host of them. And on the seventh Day God ended his work, which he made; and he rested on the seventh Day from all his work, which he made (Genesis 1:3-31 KJV).

In God's infinite wisdom, He created the absolute perfect earth in six days; all that existed, including the universe, was perfect, and God saw that it was good.

In understanding God's calendar, we must clearly understand the days of creation. In the book of Job, he gives us some insight into the calendar of God; he states, "Since times are not hidden from the Almighty, why do those who know Him see not His days?" (Job 24:1 NKJV).

The mystery God is trying to convey is He has not hidden time from us, yet we do not see time like God does. The Apostle Peter was able to give us a better understanding of what Job was trying to express by stating, "But beloved, do not forget this one thing, that with the Lord one day is as a thousand years, and a thousand years as one day" (2 Peter 3:8 NKJV). This is evidence that God has hidden the days of redemption in the days of creation.

Some theologians have stated not to take this literally but metaphorically except when trying to calculate specific prophecies, but this does not make sense if we follow proper Bible hermeneutics. Peter is emphasizing the certainty of the last days hidden in creation.

God is revealing to us that the days of creation are not 24-hour days, like in our calendar (the Gregorian calendar). Each day of creation is a thousand years, and this is where the mysteries of the days of creation and redemption are found; I would like to focus more on the days of creation and Adam to unveil this mystery.

Desmond Alexander explains that the Bible presents the divine revelation as a "meta-story" that comes from an anthology of literature, produced over centuries with an amazingly diverse genre, authorship, and even language."[3]

Kenneth Mathews writes, "'Beginning' is often paired in the Old Testament with its antonym 'end,' indicating an inclusive period of time (e.g., Job 8:7; 42:12; Ecclesiastes 7:8; Isaiah 46:10)."

"The occurrence of 'beginning' in Genesis 1:1 suggests that it has been selected because of its association with 'end.' If so, the author, as Creator-King of the cosmos, places His covenant people under His reign on earth. This reality was actual at the beginning (Genesis 1-2) and will be confirmed at the end (Revelation 21-22), as John the Apostle describes his vision of the Holy Jerusalem from heaven, a new heaven, and a new earth.

The beginning of Genesis is inaugurated and consummated throughout the Biblical narrative of Revelation. These books frame the entire Biblical storyline of God's redemptive plan for His people. This diagram will give you a better understanding of time hidden within the days of creation." [4]

The seventh day is a Sabbath. Tenth Day-Day of Sin
Adam & Eve live 930 years after sin. [5]

In the week of creation, man and the woman are created on the sixth day. They lived on the earth fulfilling what God had commanded until they sinned (Genesis 1:26-31). In the origin of Christianity, we find value and purpose in the theme of God creating people in His image.

The Bible is clear that Adam and the woman lived on the earth without sin, subduing and replenishing the earth, until they violated God's command and ate of "the tree of good and evil."

The Bible tells us God created Adam and the woman on the sixth day, for the number six is the number of man, and He rested on the seventh day. Through Scripture, we know that the seventh day is the Sabbath day. There is no mention of blood sacrifice from the sixth day to the seventh day because God rested, and we know that "one day is as a thousand years and a thousand years as one day," which indicates they lived one thousand years without sin through the Sabbath day, the seventh day.

To understand when Adam and the woman sinned, we have to look at the Bible and what the stipulations are concerning sin and the remission of sin. The Apostle Paul states, "In fact the law requires that nearly everything be cleansed with blood and without the shedding of blood there is no forgiveness" (Hebrews 9:22 NIV). This is why the author of the book of Hebrews provides the main reason why we as Christians believe that Jesus Christ died and shed His blood for the forgiveness of our sins—without the shedding of His blood, there would be no forgiveness of sin (Leviticus 17:11).

In the narrative of creation, Adam and the woman are given dominion over Eden and over the earth and are tasked to refill the earth with their descendants until they sinned. God judges them as the stewards of the earth, for they represented all of mankind in the Garden-Temple of God. Just as death came through one man by disobeying God's commandment, the redemption of man would come through Jesus Christ, the free gift of salvation through grace and righteousness.

"And unto Adam and his wife the Lord God made coats of skin, and clothed them. And the Lord God said, Behold, the man is become as one of us, to know good and evil: and now, lest he put forth his hand, and take also of the tree of life, and eat, and live forever.

Therefore the Lord God sent him forth from the Garden of Eden, to till the ground from whence he was taken. So he drove them out; and he placed at the east of the garden of Eden cherubims, and a flaming sword which turned every way, to keep them away from the tree of life," (Genesis 3:21-24 KJV).

This outlook permeates the entire message of the Bible, and the storyline gives us eschatological hope. On this point, Jür Genesis Moltmann was correct when he wrote, "From first to last, and not merely in the epilogue,

Christianity is eschatology, is hope, forward looking and forward moving, and therefore also revolutionizing and transforming the present."

"The eschatological is not one element of Christianity, but it is the medium of the Christian faith as such, the key in which everything else in it is set." [6]

The storyline progressively expands under the repeating theme of '(re)creation, fall, and redemption,' a cycle that repeats itself until the seed of the woman crushes the seed of the serpent (Genesis 1-3). This narrative is untimely fulfilled in Jesus Christ as He crushes the head of the serpent as He is crucified. Willem VanGemeren thus notes, "Creation, in a real sense, is the preamble to the history of redemption."

Then the question is, how long did Adam and Eve live before the fall? The Scriptures clearly declare that they lived at least 4,000 years; from the sixth day until the tenth day, they lived a thousand years, and the remaining three thousand years are found in the book of Exodus.

"And the Lord spoke unto Moses and Aaron in the land of Egypt saying, Speak unto all the congregation of Israel, saying, In the tenth day of this month they shall take to them every man a lamb, according to the house of their fathers, a lamb for an house: And ye shall keep it up until the fourteenth day of the same month: and the whole assembly of the congregation of Israel shall kill it in the evening." (Exodus 12:1,3,6 KJV)

In keeping with Biblical hermeneutics, Adam and Eve were created on the sixth day, and God's rest is broken on the tenth day because Adam and Eve sinned. On the tenth day, every man took a lamb to his father's house, and they kept the lamb until the fourteenth day of the same month; this is why the Bible declares, "And all that dwell upon the earth shall worship him, whose names are not written in the Book of Life of the Lamb, slain from the foundation of the earth" (Revelation 13:8). In the foreknowledge of God, He is able to show His creation grace and mercy from the beginning.

When we look at Scripture, God often speaks in symbols and types, and "The New Testament lies hidden in the Old Testament, and the Old Testament is unveiled in the New Testament."[7] Our redemption is found in creation in the Lamb that was slain because Adam and Eve sinned on the tenth day, and in following the days of creation, we ultimately see that the blood of Jesus has enough authority and power to meet all of creation's needs. Not even Satan understood the redemptive power of the Lamb hidden in the Old Testament and revealed in the New Testament in the death and resurrection of Jesus.

Augustine is often cited as the source of this famous quote, defining the meaning of the Bible, but its origin is actually from the Bible itself. After Jesus rose from the dead, He appeared to the disciples and told them: "These are the words which I spoke to you while I was still with you, that all things must be fulfilled which were written in the Law of Moses and the Prophets and the Psalms concerning me" (Luke 23:44). There are actually 937 Scripture citations from the Old Testament that are found in the New Testament."[8]

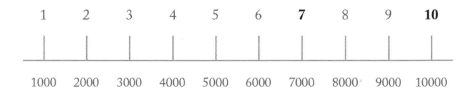

930 Years After Sin[9]

Willem VanGemeren says, "The Bible begins with the account of creation (Genesis 1:1) and ends with a description of a more glorious creation (Revelation 21-22). Organic development involves God's plan to redeem new humanity from all nations (Revelation 5:9; 7:9). Creation, in a real sense, is the preamble to the history of redemption."[10]

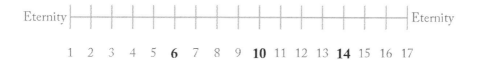

Eternity |—|—|—|—|—|—|—|—|—|—|—|—|—|—|—|—|—| Eternity

1 2 3 4 5 **6** 7 8 9 **10** 11 12 13 **14** 15 16 17

Genesis 2:1-3 Exodus 12:3, 6 Hosea 6: 1-3 The Millennium[11]

These images of calendars give a visual and a better understanding of the days of creation and redemption and the complete account of Adam and Eve, as the Bible declares they lived 4,000 years before sin and 930 years after sin.

Bible agnostics do not believe the Bible is complete because they believe its views are contradictory, and they violate the basic laws of reasoning and logic with the belief that the Bible is not 100% the words of God or inspired. Adam and Eve are commanded to "be fruitful and multiply," and then God commands them to "replenish the earth and subdue it" (Genesis 1:28). When the Bible states to "replenish the earth," they think that expression does not imply that there was a previous race of men on the earth before Adam and Eve. The word *replenish* means "to fill again." [12]

Adam and Eve enjoyed God's presence, exercised dominion over God's created order, and were tasked to re-fill the earth with their descendants. Eden is where the Biblical idea of the Kingdom is originally described in Scripture as the utopian Garden-Temple of God.

Genesis begins with a potential building site for humanity to exercise dominion, multiply, and consequently enlarge the borders of Eden: "From one man he made all the nations, that they should inhabit the whole earth; and he marked out their appointed times in history and the boundaries of their lands" (Acts 17:26).

Adam and Eve were populating the earth for 4,000 years before they sinned. They began to replenish the earth as God had commanded; Adam named his wife Eve after sin. "The man gave his wife the name 'Eve,' because she was the mother of all the living" (Genesis 3:20). "The Hebrew word study of Eve is 'Chava—Chet Vav Hei,' which means 'mother of all the living, to live or to give life.'" [13]

If we are going to look at the days of creation chronologically, Cain and Abel were Adam and Eve's first children after sin.

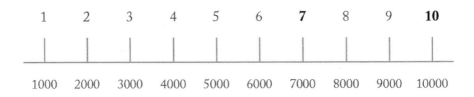

930 Years After Sin[14]

"So God created mankind in his own image, in the image of God he created them; male and female he created them. God blessed them and said to them, be fruitful and increase in number; fill (replenish, "male" means fill it again), so God is instructing Adam and Eve to fill the earth again and to subdue it. And rule over the fish in the sea and the birds in the sky and over every living creature that moves on the ground" (Genesis 1:27-28 NIV).

If Adam and Eve were the first of God's creation on the earth, why would he command them to re-fill the earth again, and name his wife Eve, which means "the mother of all the living," if Cain and Abel were their first children? Sometime after Cain kills Abel, "Cain said to the Lord, my punishment is more than I can bear.

Today you are driving me from the land, and I will be hidden from your presence: I will be a restless wanderer on the earth and whoever finds me will kill me" (Genesis 4:13-14 NIV). Who was Cain afraid of now that his brother was dead? Who would possibly be a threat to Cain on the face of the earth? Since Adam and Eve were replenishing the earth for 4,000 years,

THE ORIGIN OF SIN

Cain was afraid of his own brothers, sisters, nephews, and nieces, who would have been seeking revenge for the death of Abel.

"And again, she bore his brother Abel. Now Abel was a keeper of sheep, and Cain a worker of the ground. In the course of time Cain brought to the Lord an offering of the fruit of the ground, and Abel also brought of the firstborn of his flock and of their fat portions. And the Lord had regard for Abel; and his offering" (Genesis 4:2-4 ESV).

The Bible does not tell us their ages, but we know that they were not children but men, for they were offering their sacrifices unto the Lord, which states the age of accountability. We must also recognize that most theologians believe that Cain and Abel were both adults; it's believed that Cain was about 29 years of age, and Abel was about 22 years of age at the time that Cain kills Abel.

The Bible traces the genealogy of Seth prior to the death of his brother Abel, and it also states that Adam and Eve had other children: "The days of Adam after he fathered Seth were 800 years; and he had other sons and daughters." (Genesis 5:4 ESV).

Islam, Judaism, and Christianity trace the genealogy of the human race back to Seth: According to the Bible, God never gives any indication that Seth was Adam and Eve's first child after the death of Abel, but rather it states that he was a replacement son for the death of Abel (Genesis 4:25).

4

THE SEED OF THE WOMAN AND THE SEED OF THE SERPENT AT WAR

"And God said unto the serpent, Because thou hast done this, thou art cursed above all cattle, and above every beast of the field; upon thy belly shalt thou go, and dust shalt thou eat all the days of thy life: And I will put enmity between thee and the woman, and between thy seed and her seed; it shall bruise thy head, and thou shalt bruise his heel" (Genesis 3:14-15 KJV). God speaks to the serpent, which is the instrument the devil uses to deceive mankind, and passes judgment on the serpent. It is degraded beneath all creation and cursed to crawl upon its belly, no longer on its feet, and eat dust for the rest of its life.

Then war is proclaimed. After Adam and Eve sinned in the Garden of Eden, God made a prophetic declaration that would echo for generations to come and declared war and judgment on Satan and his seed. God, in His infinite wisdom, "knows the end from the beginning, from ancient times, what is still to come, saying my plan will be established, and I will accomplish all My good pleasure" (Isaiah 46:10 NASB).

Satan fulfilled this prophecy, as we will review further in chapters 8 and 9. This prophecy is about Satan and how God would use His creation to bring forth His Son, Jesus Christ, to give Satan the ultimate blow and bruise the head of the serpent.

Hidden in this prophetic declaration thousands of years ago in the Garden of Eden is the fact that a male child, born of a woman, a descendent of Adam, would one day defeat Satan. God the Father decided to tell Satan that the very thing he sought to corrupt in the Garden of Eden would destroy him.

Through His creation, He would create a godly bloodline that had not been corrupted, and through this bloodline, 76 generations later, a male child would be born. The Gospel of Luke gives us the genealogy of Jesus Christ: "Now Jesus himself was about thirty years old when he began his ministry. He was the son, so it was thought, of Joseph, the son of Heli" (Luke 3:23-38 NIV).

Luke gives us a very detailed outline of the genealogy of Jesus Christ. Since this prophetic declaration, Satan's primary objective was to murder or prevent this child from ever being born.

As we look further at the death of Abel through the genealogy of Cain and Seth, we will find that Abel was the chosen son that would eventually produce the Messiah but was replaced by Seth.

"Now Cain said to his brother Abel, 'Let's go out to the field.' While in the field, Cain attacked his brother Abel and killed him. Then the Lord said to Cain, 'Where is your brother Abel?' 'I don't know,' he replied, "'Am I my brother's keeper?" The Lord said, 'What have you done? Listen! Your brother's blood cries out to me from the ground'" (Genesis 4:8-10 NIV).

In his deceived state, Cain thinks he can hide his actions against his brother from God, but in the book of Genesis, Moses tells us "the blood of Abel cries out for justice" (Genesis 4:10).

The word "crying" in this verse (10) is the same word used elsewhere to speak of the pleas of those who have met injustice (Exodus 22:22-23).

I believe this was a prophetic act because the blood of Abel was crying out for all of humanity who has met injustice, crying out to our Father in heaven for the redemption of all creation. Still, God had a plan for all of humanity; He would replace Abel with his brother Seth.

From the very beginning, it has been Satan's objective to prevent the birth of the Messiah, for he knew that a male child would be born of a human woman and one day defeat him. God is merciful, and a covenant-keeping God who promised Adam and Eve a "seed" that would one day conquer Lucifer, who had deceived them to eat from "the tree of the knowledge of good and evil" (Genesis 3:6-7).

Cain showed no repentance for the death of his brother Abel; he was only concerned for his safety. Many theologians and preachers have commented and preached that Cain and Abel were the first children of Adam and Eve. But if this were true, why would Cain fear for his safety? Cain said in the Septuagint, "My Crime is too great for me to be forgiven" (Genesis 4:13 BST).

In Adam, all of mankind is represented in the beginning, and now Cain just murdered his brother Abel, representing the war between the children of God and the children of Satan. Cain's heart and mind are in a reprobate state, far from God. This is evidence of the war declared in the book of Genesis of enmity put between the seed of the woman and the seed of the serpent. Because of this, Cain's lineage would not be permitted to have fellowship with God and bring their sinful nature's influence to Seth's seed. He is cast out of Eden, put out of the presence of the Lord, and resides in the land of Nod, evidence of God's prophetic declaration in the Garden of Eden, a war between two seeds.

"And Adam knew his wife again, and she bore a son, and called his name Seth. 'For God,' said she, 'hath appointed me another seed instead of Abel, whom Cain slew.' And to Seth, to him also there was born a son; he called his name Enosh: then began men to call upon the name of the Lord" (Genesis 4:25-26 KJV).

In the Septuagint, after discussing in detail Cain's descendants through Lamech and his offspring in the previous verses, the narrative of this story comes back to the birth of Seth.

Cain is concerned about those who would take vengeance for the death of Abel, clearly suggesting that there were other people alive when he murdered his brother. Cain is cursed upon the earth and shows no remorse for the crime he's committed against his brother but complains about his punishment (Genesis 4:14).[1]

As mentioned in the previous chapter, Adam and Eve lived at least 4,000 years from the sixth day until the tenth day, which leads us to believe that Mr. and Mrs. Adam had children before Cain and Abel. The Passover is instituted, and the Israelites are instructed on how to observe the Passover (Exodus 12).

Even after the fall, Eve is still a woman of faith, trusting God that He would replace the death of her son Abel. She saw that Seth was God's replacement that would bring forth the lineage of the Messiah. "Cain said to the Lord, 'My punishment is more than I can bear. Today you are driving me from the land, and I will be hidden from your presence; I will be a restless wanderer on the earth, and whoever finds me will kill me.' But the Lord said to him, 'Not so; anyone who kills Cain will suffer vengeance seven times over.' Then the Lord put a mark on Cain (a shadow of the Antichrist) so that no one who found him would kill him." [2]

"So Cain went out from the Lord's presence and lived in the land of Nod, east of Eden. Cain made love to his wife, and she became pregnant and gave birth to Enoch. Cain then was building a city, and he named it after his son Enoch. To Enoch was born Irad, and Irad was the father of Mahujael, and Mehujael was the father of Methuselah, and Methusael was the father of Lamech" (Genesis 4:16-18 NIV). Cain's heart was filled with rebellion, and showed no remorse for what he had done to his brother, so his lineage would not be permitted to interact with the other children of Adam and Eve and have any negative, sinful influence on them.

To dwell in the land of Nod can mean to live a wandering life, and it can also mean to be a fugitive or in exile. Josephus wrote in *The Antiquities of the Jews* (a. AD 93) that Cain was destined to live the life of an outsider, alienated from God and from His presence; he lost his identity and community.

"Cain continued his wickedness in Nod, resorting to violence and robbery, establishing weights and measures, transforming human culture from innocence into craftiness and deceit, establishing property lines, and building a fortified city. Since God cursed the ground, Cain became the first real estate developer and a broker."[3]

Being in Nod meant being out of the presence of God. Many early expositors believe that Nod was the opposite of the Garden of Eden. English translations state that Nod was described as a place inhabited by ferocious beasts or monsters, the "Nephilim."

The Bible tells us that when Cain was exiled from Eden, he went "east" to the land of Nod and built a city. We are told that he named his city after his firstborn son, Enoch.

Ancient linguistics has shown that the city of Uruk in Iraq is the same word as Enoch. Etymologically speaking, the Biblical narrative moves on to Enoch, meaning "founder" in Hebrew. Enoch, a descendent of Cain, founded the first city in Mesopotamia, located in the mouth of the Euphrates River in Shinar. Historical Sumer and modern day Iraq is significant with the events of the Tower of Babel in a time when the world rebelled against God.

Archaeologists agree that this is the first city founded with Biblical accounts and built by the descendants of Cain. The city was called Eridu after Enoch's son Irad, in the land of Shinar. Shinar is mentioned eight times in the Old Testament and historically has been referred to as Babylonia, encompassing Babel, and Babylon in historical reference (Genesis 10:10 and Revelation 18:2-3).

"To Enoch was born Irad, and Irad was the father of Mehujael, and Mehujael the father of Methushael and Methushael was the father of Lamech" (Genesis 4:18 NIV). The names given in this verse of Scripture tend to focus on the genealogy of Cain. "It is believed these begat sons, that exceeded others in bulk and height, whose names were given to the mountains they first possessed, and from them were called Cassius, Libanus, Antillibanus, and Brathy; and of them were begotten Memrumus and Hypsuranuis, so called by their mothers, women, who without shame, lay with everyone they could meet with; of these came Agreus and Halius, the inventors of fishing and hunting; and these seem to answer to the generations from Cain to Lamech; and it is no wonder Moses should take no more notice of such a set of men." [4]

In the Sumerian language, the city known as Nun-ki', meaning "the mighty city," came to be known as the mighty city of Babylon.

Following Cain's genealogy, it is believed that the very first city he built through archaeological and Biblical accounts is modern-day Iraq.

Another interesting thing about the genealogy of Cain is his descendant, Lamech. He was responsible for the "Song of the Sword," and the Bible clarifies that he was the first polygamist, having two wives, Adah and Zillah.

"Lamech married two women, one named Adah and the other Zillah. Adah gave birth to Jabal; he was the father of those who lived in tents and raised livestock. His brother's name was Jubal; he was the father of all who played stringed instruments and pipes. Zillah also had a son, Tubal-Cain, who forged all kinds of tools out of [g] bronze and iron. Tubal-Cain's sister was Naamah" (Genesis 4:19-23 NIV).

The names and interpretations of Lamech's wives are very interesting. Adah, interpreted as "the deposed one," implies that Lamech spurned her in favor of Zillah, and her name means she has shaded herself at Lamech's side.

Adah was treated as an enslaved person by her husband and was at the mercy of his mistress, Zillah.

This information reveals to us the immorality that the descendants of Cain were practicing by taking part in polygamy in his generation. Cain had rebelled against God, but God is the merciful God, and He still extended his grace to Cain.

"But the Lord said to him, 'Not so, anyone who kills Cain will suffer vengeance seven times over.' The Lord put a mark on Cain so that no one who found him would kill him" (Genesis 4:15 NIV).

I believe when the sons of God came to the daughters of men, they came to the daughters of Cain, and they created stringed instruments and forged all kinds of tools (Genesis 4:19-23).

The Genealogy of Cain

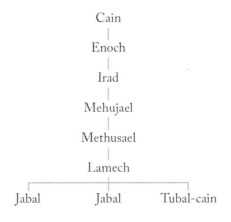

Cain
|
Enoch
|
Irad
|
Mehujael
|
Methusael
|
Lamech
|
Jabal — Jabal — Tubal-cain

5

"Adam made love to his wife again, and she gave birth to a son and named him Seth, saying, 'God has granted me another child in place of Abel, since Cain killed him.' Seth also has a son, and he named him Enosh, then began men to call upon the name of the Lord" (Genesis 4:25-26 NIV).

In the Septuagint, after discussing Cain's descendants through Lamech and his offspring in the previous verses, this story's narrative returns to Seth's birth and genealogy. According to the Septuagint, Adam was 130 years old when Seth was born, and when Seth was 105 years old, he had his first son Enosh, so Adam was 235 years old when Enosh was born. "When Seth had lived 105 years, he became the father of Enosh"(Genesis 5:6 NIV).

"After becoming Enosh's father, Seth lived 807 years and had other sons and daughters. Seth lived 912 years, and then he died" (Genesis 5:6-8). Seth is included in the genealogy of Christ. Even though there is not much said about Seth, he became the patriarch of the first family. Seth also became the progenitor of the rest of the human race and is only mentioned two additional times in the Bible; the first is to Noah's son's to give them a historical and genealogical record." [6]

"Adam, Seth, Enosh, Kenan, Mahalel, Jared, Enoch, Methuselah, Lamech, Noah"(1 Chronicles 1:1-3, NIV). And the second time is significant because it identifies him as a direct ancestor of Jesus. "The son of Enosh, the son of Seth, the son of Adam, the son of God" (Luke 3:38 AMPC). The bloodline, or the genealogy, of Seth was called the "royal" line because they believed in God and followed Him.

"The record is perfectly natural and straightforward and is intended to give both the necessary genealogical data to denote the promised lineage and the only reliable chronological framework we have for the antediluvian period of history" (Dr. Henry Morris).

"When Seth was 105 years old, he became the father of Enosh" (Genesis 5:6 NIV). Adam is 235 years old. "When Enosh lived 90 years, he became the father of Kenan" (Genesis 5:9 NIV). Adam is 325 years old. "When Kenan had lived 70 years, he became the father of Mahalalel" (Genesis 5:12 NIV). Adam is 395 years old. "When Mahalealel had lived 65 years, he became the father of Jared" (Genesis 5:15 NIV). Adam is 460 years old. "When Jared had lived 162 years, he became the father of Enoch"

(Genesis 5:18 NIV). Adam is 622 years old. "When Enoch had lived 65 years, he became the father of Methuselah" (Genesis 5:21 NIV). Adam is 687 years old, so Adam lived 308 years into the life of Enoch and died 57 years before Enoch was taken.

"Enoch walked faithfully with God; then he was no more, because God took him away" (Genesis 5:24 NIV).

"When Methuselah had lived 187 years, he became the father of Lamech" (Genesis 5:25 NIV). Adam is 874 years old, then between verse 26 and verse 27, Adam dies 56 years into the life of Lamech at the age of 930 years.

That time in the Garden when God declares war on the seed of the serpent and Cain murders Abel, God is still so faithful to Adam, Eve, and all of Creation that he replaces the death of Abel with Seth, God's replacement for an incredible lineage that would bring forth the Messiah.

And the war begins as God continues with His eternal plan to redeem man created in the image of God. The storyline continues to expand under the repeating theme of '(re) creation, fall, and redemption,' a cycle that repeats itself until the seed of the woman crushes the serpent's seed (Genesis 1-3). Willem VanGemeren thus notes, "Creation, in a real sense, is the preamble to the history of redemption." [7]

"And, history will not end until God's sovereign plan is shown that creation's 'beginnings' were initiated with a future goal intended, an eschatological purpose. Thus the prophets and the apostles could speak of the end in terms of the beginnings, 'new heavens and new earth' in Isaiah 65:17; Revelation 21:1." [8]

The Genealogy of Seth

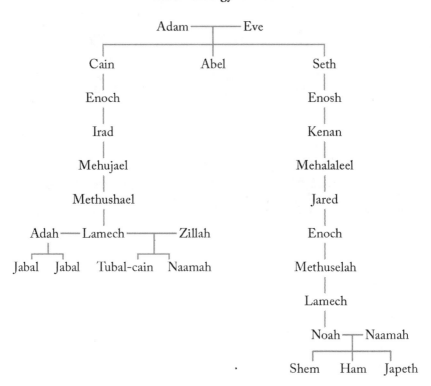

Adam ——┬—— Eve

Cain   Abel   Seth

Enoch   Enosh

Irad   Kenan

Mehujael   Mehalaleel

Methushael   Jared

Adah —— Lamech ——┬—— Zillah   Enoch

Jabal Jabal Tubal-cain Naamah   Methuselah

Lamech

Noah ——┬—— Naamah

Shem Ham Japeth

9

5

WHO WERE THE SONS OF GOD?

"And it came to pass when men began to multiply on the face of the earth, and daughters were born unto them, that the sons of God saw the daughters of men that they were fair; and they took them wives of all which they chose. And the LORD said, My spirit shall not always strive with man, for that he also is flesh: yet his days shall be a hundred and twenty years. There were giants in the earth in those days; and also after that, when the sons of God came in unto the daughters of men, and they bore children to them, the same became mighty men, which were of old, men of renown" (Genesis 6:1-4 KJV).

Satan fails with his plan to kill Abel because God replaces him with Seth, and through Seth, a new Godly lineage begins to multiply on the face of the earth. In the teachings of the Torah in the Hebrew Bible, Seth is the name of Adam and Eve's third son, which means "appointed" or "placed."

Trying to kill the man-child's birth now becomes almost impossible because Adam's descendants are growing in large numbers and subduing the earth, and Cain (an Antichrist) is no longer a threat as he is banished east of Eden to the land of Nod. We know that Adam and Eve had been subduing and multiplying the earth for about four thousand years before sin, but now that Adam and Eve sinned, the man-child must come forth from Seth's lineage, "the replacer," to redeem all of humanity back from a fallen state.

To corrupt humanity, Satan uses a plan for the "sons of God" to leave their natural habitat and look upon "the daughters of men."

In the history of the church age, it's questioned if the "sons of God" were angels or the offspring of Seth.

All the earliest documents and sources validate that the "sons of God" were angels. The Enochic literature, the Dead Sea Scrolls, the Genesis Apocrypha, the Damascus Document, and the Book of Jubilees, even though these documents are not included in the Canon, are still excellent sources for commentary purposes.

In the Septuagint, the reading "angels," found in Codex Alexandrinus, one of the four main witnesses to the Greek text, identifies the meaning of *bene ha Elohim* in Hebrew.

The phrase "sons of the Elohim" also appears in several Scriptures. "One day the angels came to present themselves before the Lord, and Satan also came with them" (Job 1:6 NIV), and "On another day the angels came to present themselves before the Lord, and Satan also came with them to present himself before him" (Job 2:1 NIV).

In both Scriptures, "angels" in Hebrew refers to the sons of Elohim. In two Dead Sea Scrolls, "the sons of Elohim," or sons of El, are referred to as "angels of God" and sometimes as "sons of God" or "sons of Israel." There is enough Biblical and commentary evidence in the Bible to conclude that when it mentions "sons of God," it is referring to angels (Genesis 6:1-4).

This is a very controversial subject within the church; many pastors don't want to preach or teach this from the pulpit. But I believe God is raising a generation of believers that will teach and preach the truth and not this watered down, cotton candy Gospel that results in believers living a lukewarm Christian life in this present age because they think living in the age of grace gives them an excuse to sin and teach and preach this false Christianity (Motivational Preaching).

The Bible teaches us that it was during the life of Adam "when man began to multiply, and the sons of God saw that the women were beautiful and took them as wives" (Genesis 6:1-4). A sect of angels rebelled against God in an attempt to destroy the seed of God by corrupting them through marriage and giving birth to giants.

As we look at the timeline of Adam's descendants, we know that Mr. and Mrs. Adam lived on the earth for about four thousand years before sin (Exodus 12).

"With this extended lifespan, as husband and wife commanded to multiply or replenish, it is evident that they conceived hundreds of children, rapidly populating the earth. In staying with the timeline of Scripture, it is clear that when the sons of God saw the daughters of men that were fair; they took them wives of which they chose" (Genesis 6:2 KJB). [1]

Now we must keep the correct timeline of these events. It does not occur until after Adam and Eve sin and continues until the days of Noah.

"The Nephilim were on the earth in those days, and afterward when the sons of God went to the daughters of humans and had children by them, they were the heroes of old, men of renown" (Genesis 6:4).

They began to multiply immediately after the command of God to multiply. "From one man he made all the nations, that they should inhabit the whole earth; and he marked out their appointed times in history and the boundaries of their lands" (Acts 17:26 NIV). Through God's sovereignty, the Apostle Paul is able to prophetically reflect on the book of Genesis through the obedience of Adam and Eve; by replenishing the earth, God made all the nations of the world.

We also know the timeline of Adam's descendants after sin because Adam lived until he was 930 years old and saw seven generations of the Messianic bloodline. Adam lived 308 years into Enoch's life and died 57 years before Enoch is taken to heaven (Genesis 5:3). The Bible tells us after the death of Abel, Adam and Eve give birth to Seth, he's created in the image of God, and all the nations of the earth are established in the image of God.

We find that the Bible does confirm that the "sons of God" were not human, but "sentient beings," and it confirms they had sexual relations with human woman. To establish the term *Elohim* in the Scriptures, it is clear that the "sons of God" are, in fact, fallen angels. In fact, Job speaks about a time when the "sons of God" were in the presence of God when He laid the foundations and fashioned a pre-Adamic world. Furthermore, the use of the term *ben nai Elohim* in the Old Testament is referring to angels.

"Where were you when I laid the earth's foundation? Tell me if you understand? Who marked off its dimensions? Surely you know! Who stretched a measuring line across it? On what were its footings set, or who laid its cornerstone, While the morning stars sang together and all the angels shouted for joy?" (Job 38:4-7 NIV).

God is asking Job, Did you witness creation "when the sons of God shouted for joy" and God was creating the "foundations of the earth"? He is using this metaphor to show Job and humanity that it is impossible to understand the mysteries of God due to the concession of our human weakness until God opens our eyes to understand the hidden things that were preserved for the end times.

"The secret things belong to the Lord our God, but the things revealed belong to us and to our children forever, that we may follow all the words of this law" (Deuteronomy 29:29 NIV). Moses is able to reveal to us that there are mysteries, "secret things," knowledge that is only known to God, but to those that follow the words of the law, He is able to reveal mysteries that belong to us.

In order to properly understand who the Nephilim were, we must have a clear understanding of who and what the Bible identifies as "the sons of God."

We examined the position of the Bible; it refers to "angels" in Greek. The Tanakh, or Old Testament, the Apocrypha, and the Kabbalah (Hebrew) are referring to the sons of Elohim.

In two Dead Sea Scrolls, they refer to "the sons of Elohim," "sons of El," or "angels of God" and sometimes "sons of God" or "sons of Israel." There is enough Biblical and commentary evidence in the Bible in reference to Genesis 6:1-4 to conclude that when it mentions "sons of God," it is referring to angels.

Some Biblical scholars refer to a school of thought as the Sethite view. We will visit this school of thought so that as we discuss the Nephilim, we will better understand Biblical history and Biblical truth.

The "generations of Adam" is recorded in the genealogical bloodline (Genesis 6:1). It is where the name "Adam's line" and the Sethite or the Canaanite streams of thought or school are birthed. The book of Genesis states that the Sethite bloodline extends to Noah and his sons. Many have been taught the history of the church age (Genesis 6) referring to the line of Seth. It was kept separate from the line of Cain and was a faithful bloodline that produced leaders in the line of Seth, called the "sons of God," and the "daughters of men" is a line of women from the line of Cain. Many have taught that this ungodly union between these two lines resulted in the offspring of the "Nephilim."

The fifth century church's lack of knowledge of the Septuagint views the interpretation of "angels" in Genesis 6 as an embarrassment when attacked by those who criticized the early church. It was about this time that the worship of angels was introduced and adopted by the church, which at the time had also become an institution of celibacy, and so the thought of angels having sex with the "daughters of men" would have significantly impacted the views they had adopted.

"Celsus and Julian the Apostate used the traditional "angel" belief to attack Christianity, Julius Africanus restored to the Sethite interpretation as a more comfortable ground. Cyril of Alexandria also repudiated the orthodox "angel" position with the "line of Seth" interpretation. Augustine also embraced the Sethite theory, and thus, it prevailed into the Middle Ages. It is still widely taught today among many churches that find the literal "angel" view disturbing. Many outstanding Bible teachers still defend this view." [2]

The Bible records the genealogy and lifespan of Adam, Noah, and Seth, and the Sethites argue their position that these are the "sons of God."

There still seems to be much controversy within the body of Christ, and many Christians defend this school of thought; if the "sons of God" were Sethites, then these Scriptures refer to the sons of Elohim.

In two Dead Sea Scrolls, "the sons of Elohim, sons of El, or it will refer to them as "angels of God" and sometimes as "sons of God" or "sons of Israel."

There is enough Biblical and commentary evidence to suggest that when the Bible in Genesis 6:1-4 mentions "sons of God" that it is referring to angels. Then what abomination did they commit that would cause them to marry the daughters of Cain and produce a new species upon the face of the earth called the Nephilim? These Watcher angels not only rebelled against God but caused creation to give themselves over to the behavior of practicing polygamy.

Those who hold this view, and believe that the Nephilim were not giants, try to connect to the Hebrew word *naphal*, meaning, "to fall," and view it as men falling from their relationship with God. These marriages between these two bloodlines of believers and unbelievers would want to annihilate the earth and prevent the Messiah from ever being born.

Noah and his family were not sinless because the Bible clearly states, "Wherefore, as by one man sin entered into the world, and death by sin; and so death passed upon all men, for that all have sinned" (Romans 5:12 KJV).

God instructed them to build an ark; their bloodline had not been contaminated with the DNA of the "sons of God."

The Book of Enoch states, "And it came to pass when the children of men had multiplied that in those days were born unto them beautiful and comely daughters. And the angels, the children of the heavens, saw and lusted after them, and said to one another: 'Come, let us choose wives from among the children of men and beget us children.'

And Semjaza, who was their leader, said unto them: 'I fear that you may not wish this deed to be done and I alone will pay for this great sin.' And they all answered him, and said: 'Let us all swear an oath, and bind one another with curses, so not to alter this plan, but to carry out this plan effectively.' Then they all swore together and all bound one another with curses to it. And they were, in all, two hundred, and they came down on Ardis, which is the summit of Mount Hermon. And they called the mountain Hermon because on it they swore and bound one another with curses" (Enoch 6:1-6).

Properly interpreting Genesis 6 states that Noah is "perfect in his generation." "These are the generations of Noah: Noah was a just man and perfect in his generation, and Noah walked with God. And Noah begat three sons, Shem, Ham, and Japheth. The earth also was corrupt before God, and the earth was filled with violence. And God looked upon the earth, and behold, it was corrupt; for all flesh had corrupted his way upon the earth" (Genesis 6:9-12 KJV).

The Book of Jasher states, "And their judges and rulers went to the daughters of men and took their wives by force from their husbands according to their choice, and the sons of men in those days took from the cattle of the earth, the beasts of the field; and the fowls of the air, and taught the mixture of animals of one species with the other, in order therewith to provoke the

Lord; and God saw the whole earth and it was corrupt, for all flesh had corrupted its ways upon earth, all men and all animals" (Jasher 4:18).

In the book of Genesis, Moses, the prophet of God, tells us, "This is the genealogy of Noah. Noah was a just man, perfect in his generations. Noah walked with God" (Genesis 6:9 KJV). The prophet Moses speaks of the "genealogy of Noah" and states that he was perfect in his generation. I believe the prophet Moses is telling us that Noah and his family were genetically pure in their generation.

The concept of a separate line contradicts Scripture and is suspect. The natural procreation of parents with different religious views will never produce an abomination like the Nephilim. If this were true today, believers marrying unbelievers would have produced unnatural offspring resulting in an abnormal creature. The Sethite view was popular until the nineteenth century, and this view dominated how Christians interpret Genesis 6.

Christians who lived in this time and those who lived in the twenty-first century should not base their belief system and understanding of Scripture on most people's opinions but must base them on sound Biblical doctrine. Throughout the history of the church, there is no valid historical account of Christians or Jews who believe this view was dominant prior to the late second and third centuries. Many have interpreted the Sethite view because, in the New Testament, believers are called "sons of God."

"For as many as are led by the Spirit of God, these are sons of God" (Romans 8:14 KJV). In this verse in the book of Romans, the Apostle Paul is writing to the church in Rome that as Christians, through faith and grace, we are to turn away from our sins through the ministry of the Holy Spirit and become mature in our faith, for "these are the sons of God."

There is also another scripture in the New Testament that the Apostle Paul wrote, "For you are all sons of God through faith in Christ Jesus" (Galatians 3:26 NKJV). To clarify "sons of God" in the New Testament, we must look at the Greek words and their translations. The word "son," translated in Greek, is *teknon* and *hulos*; both indicate sonship by the origin of one's parents. So, in essence, Paul was trying to emphasize or refer to sonship by God legally adopting us into his family.

As God's creation, we are not by nature the "sons of God" until we encounter Jesus Christ and make Him Lord over our life; only then are we adopted into His family. The Bible calls us "children of wrath" when we are outside the will of God. "All of us also lived among them at one time, gratifying the cravings of our flesh and following its desires and thoughts. Like the rest, we were by nature deserving of wrath" (Ephesians 2:3 NIV).

"So God's creations, naturally, are the children of disobedience or children of wrath" until we accept the universal Body of Christ. The full measure of this adoption will culminate at the second coming of Christ when we receive our redemptive bodies. "Not only so, but we, who have the first fruits of the Spirit, groan inwardly as we wait eagerly for our adoption to sonship, the redemption of our bodies" (Romans 8:23 NIV).

Then we will be revealed as the "sons of God." "For we must all appear before the judgment seat of Christ, so that each of us may receive what is due for the things done while in the body, whether good or bad" (2 Corinthians 5:10 NIV). As a "son of God," our character and deeds will be judged; we will have to give a report of accountability for everything we have done, and no Christian will be exempt.

This revelation is not revealed, and it is reserved until we are all judged. Throughout the church's history, understanding and interpreting Scripture is vital, and it can be devastating to try and understand Scripture without proper and sound theology. Believers have been called the "sons of God" in various Scriptures in the New Testament, but not in the same context as in Genesis 6:2.

The Hebrew term "sons of God," appears six times in the Scriptures, and in most of the references, it refers to "angels," the *bene ha elohim*, and not the children of Seth. The Sethite view is still held by many Christians today, and they use the New Testament term "son of God" to make an argument as to why they believe in the Sethite view.

For a view to be sound doctrine, it must be consistent from the book of Genesis to Revelation without any contradictions. If there are any arguments for the view, we must question the validity of the position held, even if it is a position that the early church held. The Sethite view has not and cannot defend its position. It contradicts the accurate theological interpretation of Genesis 6:1-4. It gives no room for the existence of the Nephilim or why God decided to destroy the world during Noah's time with the great deluge.

"Now the earth was corrupt in God's sight and was full of violence. God saw how corrupt the earth had become, for all the people on the earth had corrupted their ways. God said to Noah, "I am going to put an end to all the people, for the earth is filled with violence because of them. I am surely going to destroy both them and the earth" (Genesis 6:11-13 NIV).

In context, we will look at "sons of God" as referring to angels.

In our evolution as humans, it is complicated to accept that "angels" left their estate and took human wives at one time. But this is why we must become students of the Word as Christians. "Work hard so you can present yourself to God and receive his approval. Be a good worker, one who does not need to be ashamed and who correctly explains the word of truth" (2 Timothy 2:15 NLT). We need to follow basic Biblical principles and allow Scriptures to interpret Scriptures. The Scriptures also look at the unfolding of this theme in light of the Old and New Testaments; thus, the effort is Biblical theology. Under this effort, we must discover the proper Biblical teachings on the subjects.

6

ANGELS WHICH KEPT NOT THEIR FIRST ESTATE

"And the angels which kept not their first estate, but left their own habitation, he hath reserved in everlasting chains under darkness unto the judgment of the great day. Even as Sodom and Gomorrah, and the cities about them in like manner; giving themselves over to fornication, and going after strange flesh, are set forth for an example, suffering the vengeance of eternal fire" (Jude 1:6-7 KJV).

According to theological interpretation, in heaven, the word "habitation" in Greek, *oiketerion*, occurs nowhere else in the New Testament. It means a dwelling place of the body in a spirit realm native to the "angels."

We know that they sinned after they left, but most scholars think they became "dissatisfied" with their habitation, went willingly and relinquished heaven out of jealousy for God's creation. "They told them their messages were not for themselves but for you. Good News is announced to you by those who preached in the power of the Holy Spirit sent from heaven. It is all so wonderful that even the angels are eagerly watching these things happen" (1 Peter 1:12). [1]

The Bible tells us that there are some things that God reserved for the church, some of these "angels" are eagerly watching, and some became displeased, abandoned their habitation, and then saw that the women on the earth were beautiful and took them as wives.

As an act of rebellion, they left their natural habitat to fulfill the prophetic declaration of Genesis 6: an angelic invasion against creation to corrupt humanity's bloodline, to destroy the "seed of the woman."

Satan devised a plan and lured the "sons of God" into lusting after strange flesh and indulging in sexual pleasure, and this would be the ultimate snare that defiled who they were created to be, resulting in them committing such crimes of iniquity.

Satan used the sight of beautiful women to entice them with lustful desire, knowing that in their present state, they could never be given to marriage, all to alter the genetics of the human DNA. "At the resurrection, people will neither marry nor be given in marriage; they will be like the angels in heaven" (Mathew 22:30 NIV).

"The Bible does not tell exactly how many "angels" abandoned their habitation. Still, we know that only a fraction of the angelic host rebelled, not a third of the "angels" like most preachers have been preaching for years. Most theologians have preached from the book of Revelation 12:3-4 and taught that a third of the "angels" fell with Lucifer in the first angelic rebellion." [2]

The book of Revelation's apocalyptic material is written symbolically in nature, and its contents are symbolic and metaphorical; with that said, we must understand symbols and types and allow the Scriptures to interpret Scriptures. There have been four angelic rebellions: the first, "the fall of Lucifer," and the second, "the angels that did not keep their first estate," the third "Sodom and Gomorrah," the fourth "the angels who have been bound in the river Euphrates," and I believe we are in the midst of a fifth angelic invasion.

"A great sign appeared in heaven; a woman clothed with the sun, with the moon under her feet and a crown of twelve stars on her head. She was pregnant and cried out in pain as she was about to give birth. Then another sign appeared in heaven; an enormous red dragon with seven heads and ten horns and seven crowns on his head. Its tail swept a third of the stars out of the sky (heavens) and flung them to the earth" (Revelation 12:1-4 NIV).

In the study of scripture, it is essential to understand and place the meaning of "stars" in its proper contexts. Only the appropriate language in the context can give us a clear understanding of how to interpret it. In the Bible, are stars always angels?

In the book of Genesis, Moses tells us that the seed of Abraham is likened to the stars of heaven. "Then the word of the Lord came to him: This man will not be your heir, but a son who is your own flesh and blood will be your heir. He took him outside and said, look up at the sky and count the stars if indeed you can count them. Then he said to him, so shall your offspring be" (Genesis 15:4-5 NIV).

The book of Daniel tells us the stars in heaven are people.

"And they that be wise shall shine as the brightness of the firmament; and they that turn many to righteousness as the stars for ever and ever" (Daniel 12:3 KJV).

The Scriptures also tell us that Spirit-filled Christians and ministers are likened to stars in the hand of Christ: "The mystery of the seven stars that you saw in my right hand and of the seven golden lampstands is this; The seven stars are the angels of the seven churches, and the seven lampstands are the seven churches" (Revelation 1: 20 NIV).

John writes to the church in Ephesus, and he states in his letter, "To the angel of the church in Ephesus write: These are the words of him who holds the seven stars in his right hand and walks among the seven golden lampstands" (Revelation 2:1 NIV).

As we look at the proper interpretation of Revelation 12: 1-4 we can see that when John is referring to stars, he is not referring to "angels," but believers and ministers of the Gospel. Theologians and ministers of the gospel will make reference to "The Prophetic Law of Double Reference," the law of double reference mentioned in scripture refers sometimes to the prophetic word of God referring to two events simultaneously, on relating to the time and the prophecy was given, or it can be past or sometimes the future.

The book of Daniel is used as a prophetic key to unlock apocalyptic writings, which are symbolically in nature, and its contents are symbolic and metaphorical; with that said, we must understand symbols and types and allow the scriptures to interpret scriptures. As the book of Daniel has been used by scholars and has always been essential to the key of unlocking the book of Revelation, and therefore, it is important to look at the book of Daniel as a key when we unlock the apocalyptic writings in the book of Revelation.

In keeping with the integrity of the interpretation of Scripture, we must allow the Scriptures to interpret the Scriptures; as our foundational focal point of students of the Word of God, I believe there is no Biblical evidence that one third of the angels fell with Lucifer.

There are many examples of "The Prophetic Law of Double Reference," throughout the scriptures. I want to focus on a couple of scriptures in reference to the fall of Lucifer, Satan, and a third of the Angels. Revelations 12:3-4, 7-9, 6:10, and Job 38:7, are used to teach and preach that a third of the angels fell with Lucifer.

The Bible also tells us that apostate believers are likened to falling stars, as they are out of the will of God and fall from the position that God has given them as light bearers: "They are wild waves of the sea, foaming up their shame; wandering stars, for whom bleakest darkness has been reserved forever" (Jude 13 NIV).

The description here is that apostates are like stars without orbit or direction, and men at sea use stars as fixed points in navigation. So believers who fix their navigational compass on false teachers, false prophets, and doctrines of men lose their sense of orientation in their walk with God and in adequately interpreting the Scriptures.

Looking at the full context of Revelation 12:1-4, and looking at the activity of stars, this would indicate that they are not falling "angels," as many theologians, pastors, and teachers have shown. Still, they are human believers, "Christians," who are in an apostate state from the faith.

The literal falling stars are used as symbolically falling spiritual stars. "Now we beseech you, brethren, by the coming of our Lord Jesus Christ, and by our gathering together unto him, That ye be not shaken in mind, or be troubled, neither by spirit, or by word, nor by letter as from us, as that day of Christ is at hand. Let no man deceive you by any means: for that day shall not come, except there come a falling away first, and that man of sin be revealed, the son of perdition" (2 Thessalonians 2:1-3 KJB).

The word "rebellion" translated in Greek is "falling away," *apostasia*, which is where we get the English word "apostasy." It refers to a defection from your Christian faith and the one true God.

In the Scriptures, Jesus clearly warns us in the Scriptures concerning this in the last days, and it's erroneous for theologians, pastors, and teachers to try to place this end time scripture with the fall of Lucifer, which happened at the beginning of creation when he was cast out alone with NO MENTION OF FALLEN ANGELS, this position cannot be defended and it contradicts the accurate theological interpretation.

In the book of Revelation and the book of Jude, there is mention of these fallen angels who are bound in the great river Euphrates. The four angels were loosed and had been prepared to kill a third of mankind (Revelation 9:14-15).

These four angels have been kept incarcerated for six thousand years but in an hour are loosed, on an appointed day, to slay a third of mankind.

The language in this portion of scripture resembles the language of Revelation 12:4, "And his tail drew the third part of the stars of heaven, and did cast them to the earth," but in this scripture it clearly states that a third of mankind is killed.

Staying with the principle that scripture interprets scripture, we must also keep the correct timeline of these events as an end time event; as our foundational focal point of students of the Word of God, there is no Biblical evidence that one third of the angels fell with Lucifer, but this is an end time event where one third of mankind, or "stars," is killed, The great falling away is an apostate church giving themselves over to false teachings and doctrines. They will obtain forbidden knowledge, like Adam and Eve, by giving themselves over to seducing spirits. "But be doers of the word, and not hearers only, deceiving yourselves" (James 1:22 ESV).

"Thine heart was lifted up because of thy beauty, thou has corrupted thy wisdom by reason of thy brightness: I will cast thee to the ground, I will lay thee before kings, that they may behold thee. Thou has defiled thy sanctuaries by the multitude of thine iniquities, by the iniquity of thy traffic; therefore will I bring forth a fire from the midst of thee, it shall devour thee, and I will bring thee to ashes upon the earth in the sight of all them that behold thee. All they that know thee among the people shall be astonished at thee: thou shalt be a terror, and never shalt thou be any more" (Ezekiel 28:17- 19 KJV).

When we look at this scripture we immediately recognize that it's not speaking about the King of Tyre, but it is referring to Lucifer as he is cast to the earth alone as a ball of fire. In the book of Revelation, in chapter 12, when the dragon's tail draws a third part of the stars, the text is not speaking about "angels" but about the seed of father Abraham.

In using the Book of Enoch for commentary purposes only, I will quote from the book to give us a better understanding of how many "angels" abandoned their habitation in the second angelic invasion.

"And it came to pass when the children of men had multiplied that in those days were born unto them beautiful and comely daughters. And the angels, the children of heaven, saw and lusted after them, and said to one

THE ORIGIN OF SIN

another; Come, let us choose us wives from among the children of men and beget us, children.

And Semjaza, who was their leader, said unto them; I fear ye will not indeed agree to do this deed, and I alone shall have to pay the penalty of a great sin. And they all answered him and said: Let us all swear an oath, and all bind ourselves by mutual imprecations not to abandon this plan but to do this thing.

Then sware they all together and bound themselves by mutual imprecations upon it. And they were all two hundred; who descended in the days of Jared on the summit of Mount Hermon, and they called it Mount Hermon, because they had sworn and bound themselves by mutual imprecations upon it" (1 Enoch 6:7-8).

The Book of Enoch is not inspired and is not part of the canon, but this does not mean that it doesn't contain truth, the same way we read other books that have not been inspired but have been written by some of the most prolific authors of our time. We have been known to extract information pertinent to our teaching and preaching. In the same manner, we can extract relevant details from the Book of Enoch and other Apocrypha books that godly men like Peter and Jude quoted.

"For God did not spare angels when they sinned, but cast them into hell and committed them to chains of gloomy darkness to be kept until the judgment; if he did not spare the ancient world, but preserved Noah, a herald of righteousness, with seven others, when he brought a flood upon the world of the ungodly; if by turning the cities of Sodom and Gomorrah to ashes he condemned them to extinction, making them an example of what is going to happen to the ungodly; and if he rescued righteous Lot, greatly distressed by the sensual conduct of the wicked, for as that righteous man lived among them day after day, he was tormenting his righteous soul over their lawless deeds that he saw and heard; then the Lord knows how to rescue the godly from trials, and to keep the unrighteous under punishment until the day of judgment, and especially those who indulge in the lust of defiling passions and despise authority" (2 Peter 2:4-10 ESV) .

In 2 Peter 2:3 and Jude 1:6, Peter and Jude are quoting from the Book of Enoch, which is part of the pseudepigrapha, which is Christian Jewish scripture not accepted into the canon and that has been attributed to ancient heroes of the faith.

Why would Peter and Jude quote from the Book of Enoch? I believe that Peter and Jude had a revelation of these events and were quoting truth as they received revelation from God.

"When Enoch had lived 65 years, he became the father of Methuselah, after he became the father of Methuselah, Enoch walked faithfully with God for 300 years and had other sons and daughters.

Altogether, Enoch lived 365 years. Enoch walked faithfully with God; then he was no more, because God took him" (Genesis 5:21-24 NIV).

If we take a glimpse into Enoch's life and look at the phrase "walked with God," it is translated in the Septuagint *ueeresese to Theo*, meaning that he pleased God.

So walking with God implies that he communes with Him in thought, word, and deed, which presents a notable example that there was a dialogue about the things that Enoch writes, and there were events that God shared with Enoch.

The Bible does not give an exact period of when the "sons of God" abandoned their habitation and revolted against the Godhead. We know that Mr. and Mrs. Adam lived on the earth for about 4,000 years, replenishing and subduing the earth without sin, and that from the time they sinned until the days of Noah, within this period, the "sons of God" rebelled against God. This was a snare of Satan by providing a platform of temptation for sexual pleasure as the "sons of God" observed all of creation as inferior to them.

They were provoked by the lust of the flesh as their eyes gazed at the beautiful women of the earth, knowing that in their present state, they would not be able to take them as wives and have sexual relationships with them.

During the second angelic invasion, the Sons of God were angels who cohabited with the daughters of men, or the daughters of Cain to produce giants who became evil spirits. God made the whole world and subjected earthly things to man, arranging the elements of heaven for the increase of fruits and rotation of the seasons. He appointed this divine law and committed the care of men and all things under heaven to angels whom He appointed over them. The idea is that they can take possession of someone and acknowledge God's helpmate.

But the angels transgressed this appointment, captivated by the love of women, and begat children who are called Nephilim. They afterward subdued the human race to themselves, partly by magical writings, by fears and the punishments they occasioned, and by teaching them to offer sacrifices, incense, and libations. For whatever name each of the angels had given to himself and his children, by that name, they called them." [3]

From the days of the Apostles and the early church, there have been various writings and interpretations of "angels" who lusted after human women, married them, and had children by them.

We live in a generation where many call themselves Christians but do not know the Scriptures. If they have come across a conversation with someone concerning the events of Genesis 6:2, they can not understand or believe how something like this could have ever happened.

The church in America and throughout the world has got to return to teaching truth. A generation claims to have a relationship with God but has no intimacy or knowledge of God, but has given themselves to these cotton candy preachers, "False Prophets" and "False Teachers."

We must understand that scripture supports these events written by Moses under the inspiration of the Holy Spirit. "All Scripture is inspired by God and is useful to teach us what is true and to make us realize what is wrong in our lives. It corrects us when we are wrong and teaches us to do what is right. So that the man of God may be complete, fully equipped for every good work" (2 Timothy 3:16-17 NLT).

We have free will on how we want to live our Christian lives, so everyone wants to be spiritual but does not want to study the Scriptures to show that they have Biblical knowledge of the truth and are submitted to spiritual authority.

The Bible teaches us before you can hold the office of a true apostle or prophet you will have to go through a time of testing, a time of being processed. Gods will test your obedience through your finances, health, marriage and your heart. When Lucifer was in heaven going in and out of the earth the spirit of iniquity came upon him. He was being tested, for God came to test his heart, in the secrecy of his heart he wanted to be like God and he became prideful and iniquity was found in him.

As Christians living in the end times we must recognize that Satan and the principalities of the heavens is not the most dangerous opposition we face but the spirit of Anti Christ, which is the spirit of iniquity. The spirit of iniquity will come and attack you before the son of perdition is revealed through dreams and visions, to test your heart before you are elevated to the office of an apostle or prophet to accomplish your assignment on earth, for promotion comes from the Lord (2 Thessalonians 2:7).

7

THE NEPHILIM

"The Nephilim were on the earth in those days and also afterward—when the sons of God went to the daughters of humans and had children by them. They were the heroes of old, men of renown" (Genesis 6:4 NIV).

The Nephilim are the by-product of "angels" that the Hebrew Bible defines as the "sons of God" who married the daughters of Cain and produced this abomination called giants, "the fallen ones." The *rephaim* are names given to describe them in the Hebrew Bible.

The word Nephilim, when translated into the English language, means "fallen ones." These "fallen ones" started mixing with the human race, and I believe, starting with the line of Cain, forming an alliance that gave birth to these giants.

"So Cain went out from the Lord's presence and lived in the land of Nod, east of Eden. Cain made love to his wife, and she became pregnant and gave birth to Enoch. Cain was then building a city, and he named it after his son Enoch, To Enoch was born Irad, and Irad was the father of Mehujael, and Mehujael was the father of Methushael, and Methushael was the father of Lamech. Lamech married two women, one named Adah and the other Zillah. Adah gave birth to Jabal; he was the father of all who played stringed instruments and pipes. Zillah also had a son, Tubal-Cain, who forged all kinds of tools out of bronze and iron. Tubal-Cain's sister was Naamah" (Genesis 4:16-22 NIV).

"To dwell in the land of Nod can mean to live a wandering life, and it can also mean to be a fugitive. Josephus wrote in *The Antiquities of the Jews* (a. AD 93) that Cain continued his wickedness in Nod: resorting to violence and robbery; establishing weights and measures; transforming human culture from innocence into craftiness and deceit; establishing property lines and building a fortified city."[1]

Being in Nod meant being out of God's presence; many early expositors tend to believe that Nod was the opposite of the Garden of Eden. English tradition states Nod is described as a place inhabited by "ferocious beasts or monsters, Nephilim."

The Bible tells us that when Cain was exiled from Eden, he went "east" to the land of Nod and built a city. We are told that he named his city after his firstborn son, Enoch. Ancient linguistics has shown that the city of Uruk, in Iraq, is the same word as Enoch, etymologically speaking. So the Biblical narrative moves on to Enoch, meaning "founder" in Hebrew, saying that he founded the first city in Mesopotamia, located in the mouth of the Euphrates River in Shinar, which is historical Sumer and modern-day Iraq.

Archaeologists agree that this is the first city founded with Biblical accounts and built by the descendants of Cain. The city was called Eridu after Enoch's son Irad.

"To Enoch was born Irad, and Irad was the father of Mehujael, and Mehujael the father of Methushael and Methushael was the father of Lamech" (Genesis 4:18 NIV).

In the Sumerian language, the city was known as Nun-ki', meaning "the mighty city," later became known as the mighty city of Babylon.

Following Cain's genealogy, archaeologists believe that the first city he built, through archaeological and Biblical accounts, is modern-day Iraq. As we look at the lineage of Cain, there is a direct correlation to the birth of the Nephilim.

"And Cain knew his wife, and she conceived, and bare Enoch: and he builds a city, and called the name of his son, Enoch" (Genesis 4:17 KJV).

We know that Adam and Eve had been subduing and multiplying replenishing the earth for about 4,000 years before sin, but now that Adam and Eve had sinned, the earth was full of their descendants, and this is where Cain's wife comes from. She is a daughter of Adam and Eve and not a daughter of Abel, and there is no Biblical account of Abel ever having a wife and conceiving children.

Many Bible scholars have pondered where Cain's wife came from; the most direct Biblical evidence is that she was his sister. Revolting as this may sound because of the societies that we have grown up in that have attached a stigma to incest, the answer is clear that she was his sister.

"The man called his wife's name Eve (Chava) because she was the mother of all living" (Genesis 3:20 ESV). "According to the Jewish mystical tradition, there are three main concepts connected to the Hebrew name Chavah. The first comes from the explanation given in the Torah itself: because she is *em kol chai* - the mother of all life, or mother of all living." [2]

When man began to multiply on the earth, the Bible allowed the marriage of family members; the law against marrying between close relations was initiated 2,500 years after Adam and Eve were created under the Mosaic Law.

"According to various Abrahamic traditions, Awan (also Avan or Aven, meaning "vice" or "potency" in Hebrew) was the wife and sister of Cain and the daughter of Adam and Eve."

When we dig a little deeper into the meaning of Cain's wife's name, it means iniquity, immoral or grossly unfair behavior, and a form of wickedness where there is an absence of spiritual value and lawlessness. Cain, the fugitive, wanders the earth and marries his sister, Awan, who is grossly immoral in behavior and has rebelled against God. They establish a covenant and form a family that the "sons of God" can manipulate to fall prey to their angelic seduction.

The Bible tells us that "Cain was building a city, and he named it after his son Enoch, To Enoch was born Irad, and Irad was the father of Mehujael, and Mehujael was the father of Methushael, and Methushael was the father, Lamech. Lamech married two women, one named Adah and the other Zillah. Adah gave birth to Jabal; he was the father of all who played stringed instruments and pipes. Zillah also had a son, Tubal-Cain, who forged all kinds of tools out of bronze and iron. Tubal-Cain's sister was Naamah" (Genesis 4:17-22 NIV).

The Bible declares that Cain was the builder of the first city. Where did Cain learn how to build a city, and where did his sons learn how to make stringed instruments, pipes, and tools of bronze and iron?

As we discuss this in more detail, I will again use the Book of Enoch for commentary purposes to shed light on how Cain and his family obtained the knowledge and skill to build a city with tools of bronze and iron. There are many types of commentaries, and some may shed more light on a particular subject than others. All commentaries are not equal but are used to explain the view of the person reading the commentary.

"And Azazel taught men to make swords, and knives, and shields, and breastplates, and made known to them the metals of the earth and the art of working them, and bracelets, and ornaments, and the use of antimony, and the beautifying of the eyelids, and all kinds of costly stones, and all two coloring tinctures. And there arose much godlessness, and they committed fornication, and they three were led astray and became corrupt in all their ways. Semjaza taught enchantments and root-cuttings, 'Armaros the resolving of enchantments, Baraqijal (taught) astrology, Kokabel the constellations, Ezeqeel the knowledge of the clouds, Araqiel the signs of the earth, Shamsiel the signs of the sun, and Sariel the course of the moon" (Enoch 8:1-3).

We know that Cain was the firstborn of Adam after sin and was a farmer. "Agriculture is the science, art and practice of cultivating plants and livestock. Agriculture was the key development in the rise of sedentary human civilization, whereby farming of domesticated species created food surplus that enabled people to live in cities." [3] Most people view Cain as the murderer of Abel. Still, very few identify him as the first farmer, the founder of the first city, and the initiator of sacrifice—a man known to have men in his city that invented the arts.

There is no Biblical evidence that Cain possessed the skill to build the city of Enoch with only agricultural skills. Men in this city developed skills with the help of the "sons of God" and their offspring, the Nephilim.

The book of Ezekiel is the third of the latter prophets in the Tanakh and one of the major prophetic books in the Old Testament, following Isaiah and Jeremiah. [4]

The prophet Ezekiel tells us, "With thy wisdom and with thine understanding thou has gotten thee riches, and hast gotten gold and silver into thy treasures: By thy great wisdom and by thy traffic has thou increased thy riches, and thine heart is lifted up because of thy riches" (Ezekiel 28:4-5).

In studying the fall of Lucifer and the "sons of God," we find that in the Bible and in the Book of Enoch, the same language is used to refer to the corruption of humanity by enticing them with precious metals and trade— the knowledge that was only available to them because of these celestial beings.

In the pre-Adamic world of Genesis 1:1, we see that Lucifer used the same methods to corrupt humanity as the "sons of God."

The Watchers and the descendants of Cain are now beginning to launch the next phase of the seed of the woman attack now that they have given Cain the knowledge, skills, and material for building cities, making weapons, and acquiring wealth through trade.

"That the sons of God saw the daughters of men that they were fair; and they took them wives of all which they chose" (Genesis 6:2 KJV).

Cain's family willingly participated in an ungodly act with the angels and produced the Nephilim. This is crucial as we continue to look into the existence of the Nephilim.

The church has never really preached or taught on this topic due to thousands of years of religion, traditions of man, and denominations as we approach the last days and look at the days of creation and redemption. According to Hebrew traditions started at the time of creation, which put us in the year 5784, in theory, metaphorically and allegorically speaking looking at the dispensation of time, there would be only 216 years until the culmination of 6,000 years, according to the Jewish calendar.

"But of that day and hour no one knows, not even the angels of heaven, but My Father only" (Matthew 24:36 NKJV). The mystery of the redemption of time, or the second coming of Christ, is hidden in the days of creation.

As we continue to break ground by diving deeper into everything explored, we will continue to examine the Word of God and break away from tradition, religion, and denominations and use Biblical references, commentaries, and Jewish history to investigate truth as we journey through the Scriptures.

Through the apocryphal Book of Enoch, we have some understanding of how humanity obtained knowledge of various trades, arts, weapons, and even occult practices.

"Moreover, Azazel taught men to make swords, knives, shields, breastplates, the fabrication of mirrors, and the workmanship of bracelets and ornaments" (Enoch 8:1).

In this present time and age, the church is more religious, and Christians, pastors, apostles, and teachers want to accept part of the Biblical events as truth because of a lack of understanding rather than accepting it as the inspired Word of God.

"But false prophets also arose among the people, just as there will be false teachers among you, who will secretly bring in destructive heresies, even denying the Master who bought them, bringing upon themselves swift destruction" (2 Peter 2:1 ESV).

"And now your servant says, May the word of my Lord the king secure my inheritance, for my Lord the king is like an angel of God, in discerning good and evil. May the Lord your God be with you. Then the king said to the woman, Don't keep from me the answer to what I am going to ask you. Let my Lord king speak, the woman said. The king asked, isn't the hand of Joab with you in all this? The woman answered, As surely as you live, my Lord the king, no one can turn to the right or to the left from anything my Lord the king says. Yes, it was your servant Joab who instructed me to do this and who put all these words into the mouth of your servant. Your servant Joab did this to change the present situation. My Lord has wisdom like that of an angel of God, he knows everything that happens in the land" (2 Samuel 14:17-20 NIV).

Here we have a different occasion where humans receive knowledge from angels when this woman, Tekoah, compares King David's wisdom to that of celestial beings or angels. He could discern and have insight into the political realm, government, and civil matters at a height that deserves the complement of "the wisdom of angels," which gives us the inclination that knowledge from angels was imparted to humanity.

In the book of Exodus, there is evidence that the men who constructed the tabernacle received divine revelation and wisdom through the Holy Spirit. Moses had some knowledge that he had obtained from the Egyptians on how to make bricks and work with clay, but when he got into the art of cutting diamonds and molding gold, the Bible tells us he did not know a jeweler or goldsmith.

"And I have filled him with the spirit of God, in wisdom, and in understanding, and in knowledge, and in all manner of workmanship" (Exodus 31:3 NIV).

Skills in art, jewelry, gold, and bronze are all gifts from God that have been passed down to humanity through angels. Today, God is still dispensing various gifts to His body, the church.

"Now concerning spiritual gifts, brethren, I do not want you to be ignorant: You know that you were Gentiles, carried away to these dumb idols, however you were led. Therefore I make known to you that no one speaking by the Spirit of God calls Jesus accursed, and no one can say that Jesus is Lord except by the Holy Spirit. There are diversities of gifts, but the same Spirit. There are differences of ministers, but the same Lord, And there are diversities of activities, but the same God who works all in all. But the manifestation of the Spirit is given to each one for the profit of all: for to one is given the word of wisdom through the Spirit, to another the word of knowledge through the same Spirit, to another faith by the same Spirit, to another gifts of healing by the same Spirit, to another the working of miracles, to another prophecy, to another discerning of spirits, to another different kinds of tongues, to another the interpretation of tongues. But one and the same Spirit works all these things, distributing to each one individually as He will" (1 Corinthians 12:1-11 NKJV).

The early Church was full of divine spiritual gifts; throughout the church's history, some of these gifts ceased during the "Apostolic Age," and some have lingered for centuries, even to our present day. The Bible provides clear evidence of gifts and knowledge being shared or imparted to humanity through angels or the Holy Spirit.

The evidence is in Scriptures from the beginning of time; angels have been imparting knowledge to humanity as a form of trade for the daughters of men. We will continue to dive into the existence of the Nephilim.

This "angelic invasion," both in the Bible and other non-Biblical texts, suggests that this invasion was in the timeline of the days of Jared. "And they were in all two hundred; who descended in the days of Jared on the summit of Mount Hermon" (1 Enoch 6:6).

There is some compelling truth concerning Mount Herman, which marks the Promised Land's northern borders. "This land extended from Aroer on the rim of Arnon Gorge to Mount Sirion (that is, Hermon)" (Deuteronomy 4:48 NIV). According to historical events, the Sidonians knew Mount Hermon as home; they called it Mount Sirion, and the Amorites called it Senir: "The Sidonians call Hermon Sirion, while Amorites call it Senir" (Deuteronomy 3:9 ESV). Sardinians were the inhabitants of Sido; it is also known as the birthplace of Jezebel, the Phoenician princess.

"He not only considered it travail to commit the sins of Jeroboam son of Nebat, but he also married Jezebel the daughter of Ehtbaal king of the Sidonians, and began to serve Baal and worship him" (1 Kings 16:31 NIV).

The mountain in which the Nephilim descended is also considered a sacred mountain, where ancient sanctuaries have been found. It has also been called the mountain Baal Hermon because of the worship of Baal.

"These are the nations of the five lords of the Philistines and all the Canaanites and the Sidonians and the Hivites who lived on Mount Lebanon, from Mount Baal-Hermon as far as Lebo-Hamath" (Judges 3:3 ESV).

It is also known as the place Moses defeated Og, the King of Bashan, before being prohibited from crossing the Jordan River into the Promised Land.

"So at that time we took from these two kings of the Amorites the territory east of the Jordan, from the Arnon Gorge as far as Mount Hermon. (Hermon is called Sirion by the Sidonians; the Amorites call it Senir.) We took all the towns on the plateau and all Gilead, and all Bashan as far as Salekah and Edrei, towns of Og's Kingdom in Bashan. (Og king of Bashan was the last of the Rephaites. His bed was decorated with iron and was more than nine cubits wide. It is still in Rabbah of the Ammonites" (Deuteronomy 3:8-11 NIV).

Many Bible scholars debate whether Mount Hermon or the Jordan River is where the sons of God descended from the heavens to the earth for the daughters of men. Still, these locations are both known for numerous supernatural events between heaven and the earth and may have served as portals.

It is also here that Peter declared Jesus was "the Christ, the Son of the living God" (Matthew 16:16 ESV).

Mount Hermon may have also been where the transfiguration occurred when Jesus appeared in His heavenly glory (Matthew 17:1-9).

Today, the mountain where the Watchers descended is called by the Arabian people *Jabel Atalg*, which means "the snow mountain," and more than twenty temples have been found in the mountain, indicating the Nephilim's dominance in this region with their descendants.

So, Mount Hermon was likely an entry point or portal for the invasion of the Watchers so they could descend upon the face of the earth to corrupt God's creation through genetic manipulation (DNA), creating a new species, "the Nephilim."

8

A NEW SPECIES ALTERS THE DNA OF GOD'S CREATION

"And God said, Let the earth bring forth grass, the herb yielding seed, and the fruit tree yielding fruit after his kind, whose seed is in itself, upon the earth: and it was so. And the earth brought forth grass, and herb yielding seed after his kind, and the tree yielding fruit, whose seed was in itself, after his kind: and God saw that it was good, And God said, Let the earth bring forth the living creature after his kind, cattle, and creeping thing, and beast of the earth after his kind: and it was so. And God made the beast of the earth after his kind, and cattle after their kind, and everything that creepeth upon the earth after his kind: and God saw that it was good" (Genesis 1:11-12 KJV).

At the beginning of creation, in the week of creation, God instituted a genetic order—everything that He created will reproduce after its own kind. He wanted His creation to maintain a genetic order that had His fingerprint, as He established it to maintain genetic integrity.

As we explore and look deeper into this portion of the Scriptures, I believe there is some hidden truth here. "And the earth brought forth grass, and herb yielding seed after his kind, and the tree yielding fruit, whose seed was in itself, after his kind: and God saw that it was good" (Genesis 1:12 KJV)

When we first look at this portion of scripture, we want to classify it as three types of vegetation, grass, herbs, and fruits, but in the world of botany, it is classified into two groups: the "herb" and "fruit." Botany, also known as plant science or biology, comes from the Greek Word *botane*, meaning pasture.

"In the last two decades of the 21st century, botanists exploited the techniques of molecular genetic analysis including Genesisomics and proteomics and DNA sequences in the life of herbs and fruits."[1]

When we look at the Word of God collectively and look at the phrase "for it to reproduce after its kind," from the very beginning, we know that God makes a prophetic declaration and a decree that every species is to follow the divine order of the origin of creation and not mix with other species: "God made the wild animals according to their kinds, the livestock according to their kind, and all the creatures that move along the ground according to their kinds. And God saw that it was good" (Genesis 1:25 NIV).

God has placed great emphasis on maintaining the order He created for the vegetation, animals, and man, who He created "in His image" to maintain DNA integrity. "DNA, or deoxyribonucleic acid, is a molecule composed of two polynucleotide chains that coil around each other to form a double helix carrying genetic instructions for the development, functioning, growth, and reproduction of all known organisms and many viruses."[2]

"The information in DNA is stored as a code made up of four chemical bases: adenine (A), guanine (G), cytosine (C), and thymine (T). Human DNA consists of about 3 billion bases, and more than 99 percent of those bases are the same in everyone."[3]

DNA bases pair up with each other, A with T and C with G, to form units called base pairs. Each base is also attached to a sugar molecule and a phosphate molecule.

THE ORIGIN OF SIN

The sequence order of these bases determines the information available for building and maintaining an organism, similar to how letters of the alphabet appear in a specific order to form words and sentences.

Together, a base, sugar, and phosphate are called a nucleotide. Nucleotides are arranged in two long strands forming a double helix spiral.

The structure of the double helix is somewhat like a ladder, with the base forming the vertical side pieces of the ladder. An important property of DNA is that it can replicate or make copies of itself. Each strand of DNA in the double helix can serve as a pattern for duplicating the sequence of bases.

This is critical when cells divide because each new cell needs to have an exact copy of the DNA present in the old cell. "There are 58 verses in the Bible that speak of the characteristic of the human DNA, and it's the human scientific fingerprint of God on his creation."[4]

"For you created my inmost being; you knit me together in my mother's womb. I praise you because I am fearfully and wonderfully made; your works are wonderful, I know that full well" (Psalms 139:13-14 NIV).

In the book of Psalms, David lets us look into the genetic disposition of the characteristic of the human DNA, as he was formed in his mother's womb.

Man has tried to deny the existence of God from the beginning of time. Still, the bottom line is throughout all creation and nature, confirming that man's origin and development are interwoven in nature and made in the "image of God."

When we look at the Word of God, we see the mystery of how God was able to reveal to David "key characteristics of the human embryology."

During the time in which David lived, we must remember the development of modern science and technology was not present to understand the facet of human development in a mother's womb. In the nineteenth century, the scientific community was able to determine how embryos formed through the use of microscopy.

God gave David this insight almost 3,000 years ago, and he glorified God's creative process in the womb at the beginning of their relationship, which formed an intimacy knowing that the Creator of the universe handcrafted him by knitting him together through the existence of DNA.

The Bible and God's design of humanity put these "dimensions" in scripture so that no one can deny He is our Creator. "The way He did this is by using the number 23 (the chromosomes we receive from each parent) and 46 (the total number of chromosomes in our DNA that make up every cell of our bodies) to describe many things that relate perfectly to our DNA.

The number of chromosomes in the DNA of our bodies wasn't discovered until 1956. So one can't say that these numbers were used in the Bible because of this fact, but that God used these numbers in a Bible written long before the innermost building block of the human form was known to show us that He was the one who created us and that His works are always perfect." [5]

When we study the Bible in its original form, we know that the two languages are Hebrew and Greek. The Hebrew alphabet has 22 letters in the Old Testament, and the Greek alphabet has 24 letters in the New Testament, which equals a total of 46, the number of chromosomes the human body has in every DNA cell.

"The Word of God is made up of letters, so the most fundamental part of a word are letters that make up that word in the respective alphabet." [6]

John gives us a glimpse of this truth in the book of John: "In the beginning was the Word, and the Word was with God, and the Word was God" (John 1:1 NKJV).

The incredible truth about the WORD is that it shows up 1,180 times in the Bible. If you look up 1180 in Strong's Hebrew Concordance (because we are relating this to the Old Testament), the definition of H1180 is "my master, or Jehovah"! This is confirmation of the scripture above in John 1:1; "the Word was God." [7]

"The exciting thing about DNA is that to make a complete set of chromosomes by each parent, you must have 23. There is only 1 sex chromosome by each parent given to each set of 22 chromosomes to make up our 46 chromosomes DNA.

This means that the number 22 in terms of DNA can be characterized not by reproductive flesh but only as an IDEA, WORDS, or SUBSTANCE before it is given the final sex chromosome to make it capable of designing/reproducing a human form."[8]

A surprising finding, but we are about to go a little deeper into the mysteries of DNA and chromosomes. In 1978, a man named Ron Wyatt discovered the Ark of the Covenant. He found the Ark hiding in a grotto of a cave underneath the crucifixion place of Jesus. Above the Ark on the cave ceiling was a blood-stained portion of rock."

"Wyatt discovered that blood flowed down into the grotto from a crack in the ceiling reaching from the Cross staked in the ground and onto the Ark when Jesus was crucified. Laboratory tested, they discovered that the blood only had 24 chromosomes! This means that Jesus' blood had 23 chromosomes from his mother, Mary (the seed of the woman), and only 1 chromosome from His Father (God)! 23+1=24."[9]

No other human has had a blood profile like this in the history of humankind! Indeed, this was the blood of Jesus discovered on that day.

"And the Word was made flesh, and dwelt among us, (and we beheld his glory, the glory as of the only begotten of the Father,) full of grace and truth" (John 1:14 ESV).

God created Adam and Eve in His image and made a prophetic declaration in the book of Genesis: "I will put enmity between you and the woman, and between your offspring and her offspring; he shall bruise your head, and you shall bruise his heel" (Genesis 3:15 ESV).

He designed all creation in "His image" with His genetic disposition so that no one could ever question who our Creator was and is.

Lucifer is given a glimpse of what is to come. He devises a plan to alter the DNA of God's creation: he will create a new species on the earth to annihilate "man in the image of God" and destroy the "seed of the women," the "Messiah." The plan of salvation for humanity and redemption is being threatened. The Nephilim were raining havoc upon the face of the earth.

"The Nephilim were on the earth in those days and also afterward when the sons of God went to the daughters of humans and had children by them. They were the heroes of old men of renown.

The Lord saw great the wickedness of the human race had become on the earth, and that every inclination of the thoughts of the human heart was only evil.

The Lord regretted that he had made human beings on earth, and his heart was deeply troubled. So the Lord said,

'I will wipe from the face of the earth the human race I have created and with them the animals, the birds and the creatures that move along the ground for I regret that I have made them'" (Genesis 6:4-7 NIV).

The earth became wicked 6,000 years ago as Satan declared war on the "seed of the woman" and all of humanity, and a group of angels broke rank and their alliance to God in an all-out assault against His creation, contaminating the human gene pool.

In the book of Job, found in the Hebrew Bible (Tanak), which is the first poetic book in the Old Testament, it states, "If God does not trust his own angels and has charged his messengers with foolishness" (Job 4:18 NLT). I believe the Bible gives us evidence in this scripture that the creatures of heaven and the different ranks within the sentient beings that exist in the heavens created by God have free will. So what is free will? "Free will is the condition of thinking by virtue of which each of us (or angels) can determine the scope of their action with total autonomy." [10]

Angels are given the ability to choose! Humanity's DNA has been corrupted, and now there is war upon the face of the earth between two bloodlines.

"When human beings began to increase in number on the earth and daughters were born to them, the sons of God saw that the daughters of humans were beautiful, and they married any of them they chose" (Genesis 6:1-2 NIV).

The "sons of God" married the daughters of Adam, they had children, and the by-product of this abomination altered the DNA of God's creation. These children (a new species) were called the Nephilim, "the mighty men who were of old, the men of renown."

These men and their generation had become wicked sexually, and the intents of their hearts were evil.

"Now the earth was corrupt in God's sight, and the earth was filled with violence. And God saw the earth, and behold, it was corrupt, for all flesh had corrupted their way on the earth. And God said to Noah, I have determined to make an end of all flesh, for the earth is filled with violence through them. Behold, I will destroy them with the earth" (Genesis 6:11-13 ESV).

As we look into the days of Noah, the Bible tells us that God was "determined to make an end of all flesh."

Why would God want to destroy the whole animal kingdom and instruct Noah which animals to allow in the Ark?

As I have stated, I am using the Book of Enoch, the Book of Jasher, and the Book of Jubilees only for commentary and historical purposes. They are not canon and part of the Bible.

"And it came to pass when the children of men began to multiply on the face of the earth and daughters were born unto them, that the angels of God saw them on a certain year of this jubilee, that they were beautiful to look upon; and they took themselves wives of all whom they chose, land they bare unto them sons and they were giants.

And lawlessness increased on the earth and all flesh corrupted its way, alike men and cattle and beast and bird and everything that walks on the earth all of them corrupted their ways and their orders, and they began to devour each other, and lawlessness increased on the earth and every imagination of the thoughts of all men (was) thus evil continually.

And God looked upon the earth, and behold it was corrupt, and all flesh had corrupted its order, and all that were upon the earth had wrought all manner of evil before His eyes. And He said that He would destroy man and all flesh upon the face of the earth, which He had created. But Noah found grace before the eyes of the Lord. And against the angels whom He had sent upon the earth, He was exceedingly wroth, and He gave commandment to root them out of all their dominion, and He made us to bind them in the depths of the earth, and behold they are bound in the midst of them, and are (kept) separate" (Jubilees 5:1-6).

When we look at the book of Genesis in the Bible, and we read Genesis 6:1-8, we find the same language as in the Book of Jubilees; it tells of what happened in the days of Noah but is a bit more descriptive, shedding more light onto the events of "the days of Noah."

Looking into the days of Noah, the Bible tells us that all flesh had become evil (corrupted), and "He regretted that He had made man and with them all the animals, the birds and the creatures that move along the ground, for I regret that I have made them" (Genesis 6:7).

"Now the earth was corrupt in God's sight and was full of violence. God saw how corrupt the earth had become, for all the people on the earth had corrupted their ways. So God said to Noah, I am going to put an end to all people, for the earth is filled with violence because of them. I am surely going to destroy both them and the earth" (Genesis 6:11-13 NIV).

All of humanity is threatened because the genetic DNA of man, the animal kingdom, and the underwater kingdom have been corrupted, causing extreme violence and threatening the seed of the woman.

When we look up the word "corrupted" in Genesis 6:11, under the Strong's *Concordance* number H7843, we find the translation *shchath*, which means "to be marred, be spoiled, be corrupted, be ruined."

If we look at Genesis 13:10, it is the same language used in the days of Sodom and Gomorrah. The giants had jeopardized and damaged the genetic pool on the earth, creating new species that were an abomination in the sight of God.

"And all the sons of men departed from the ways of the Lord in those days as they multiplied upon the face of the earth with sons and daughters, and they taught one another their evil practices and they continued sinning against the Lord. And every man made unto himself a god, and they robbed and plundered every man, his neighbor as well as his relative, and they corrupted the earth, and the earth was filled with violence.

And their judges and rulers went to the daughters of men and took wives by force from their husbands according to their choice, and the sons of men in those days took from the cattle of the earth, the beasts of the field and the fowls of the air, and taught the mixture of animals of one species with the other, in order therewith to provoke the Lord; and God saw the whole earth and it was corrupt, for all flesh had corrupted its ways upon earth, all men and all animal. And the Lord said, I will blot man that I created from the face of the earth, yea from and to the birds of the air, together with cattle and beasts that are in the field for I repent that I made them. And all men who walked in the ways of the Lord, died in those days, before the Lord brought the evil upon man which he had declared, for this was from the Lord, that they should not see the evil which the Lord spoke of concerning the sons of men.

And Noah found grace in the sight of the Lord, and the Lord chose him and his children to raise up seed from them upon the face of the whole earth" (Jasher 4:16-21).

Using the Book of Jasher, for historical and commentary purposes, to make an analytical comparison with Genesis 6:11-13, we can again see that the language is the same. Still, the Book of Jasher tells us about the "sons of men" or "the sons of God."

They took from the cattle of the earth, the beasts of the field, fowls of the air, and creatures of the sea and taught the mixture of animals of one species with the other, in order therewith to provoke the Lord. To break it down into a language that can be understood, there were "human hybrids" upon the face of the earth.

Many theologians, scholars, and religious people would call this heresy, but we must allow the Scriptures to be interpreted. We cannot choose what we believe in the Bible; we either accept the whole Word of God or we don't.

The evidence of human and angel hybrids is not the only evidence of hybrids in the Bible. There were also human and animal hybrids on the earth in those days. The word "satyr" is mentioned twice in the Bible: "But wild beasts of the desert shall lie there; and their houses shall be full of doleful creatures; and owls shall dwell there, and *satyrs* shall dance there" (Isaiah 13:21 KJV).

And the second time that it appears in the Bible is also in the book of Isaiah.

"The wild beasts of the desert shall also meet with the wild beasts of the island, and the "*satyr*" shall cry to his fellow; the screech owl also shall rest there, and find for herself a place of rest" (Isaiah 34:14 KJV).

Theologians, and scholars will say that because of the subtle and rich development of the English language and how it is reflected in the King James translation in the Word of God, the translation of words is sometimes used in association with another word to give it a different meaning. They would tell you that "the word in the two Isaiah passages" in the Hebrew translation, according to most recent dictionaries, has a definition of meaning "hairy," and they want to apply it to a description of Esau, the "he-goat" in the book of Genesis.

"And Jacob said to Rebekah his mother, Behold, Esau, my brother is a hairy man, and I am a smooth man" (Genesis 27:11 KJB).

When we look up the word "satyrs" in Isaiah 13:21 and 34:14 under the Strong's *Concordance* number H8163, we find the translation means the following: kid (28), goat (24), devil (2), satyr (2), hairy (2), rough (1). Satyr may also refer to a demon-possessed goat like the swine of Gadara (Matthew 8:30-32).

Looking at the root word "etymology" in Strong's *Concordance* H8175, it means "to be horribly afraid, fear, hurled as a demon, tempestuous."

According to the dictionary, "etymology" studies the origin of words and how their meanings have changed throughout history.

"'Etymology' are not definitions; they're explanations of what our words meant and how they sounded 600 or 2,000 years ago." [11]

To be consistent, we must let the scripture interpret the Scriptures as we look at the book of Genesis and Noah and the flood: "Now the earth was corrupt in God's sight and was full of violence. God saw how corrupt the earth had become, for all the people on earth had corrupted their ways. So God said to Noah, I am going to put an end to all people, for the earth is filled with violence because of them. I am surely going to destroy both of them on the earth" (Genesis 6:11-13 NIV).

The Bible is clear that there was a mixture of humans and animals. Knowing that there was a mixture of animal and human hybrids, we look at the word "satyr" in Greek mythology, which means "one of a class of lustful, drunken woodland gods.

In Greek art, they were represented as a man with a horse's ears and tail, but in Roman representations as a man with a goat's ears, tail, legs, and horns. Satyrs were characterized by their ribaldry and were known as lovers of wine, music, dancing, and women." [12]

One thing for sure is that the Bible is clear that there were human hybrids in those days, and in the book of Jude, they were going after "strange flesh": "In like manner, Sodom and Gomorrah and the cities around them, who indulged in sexual immorality and pursued strange flesh, are on display as an example of those who sustain the punishment of eternal life" (Jude 1:7).

At this point, the survival of all humanity is threatened, and Lucifer has waged war on the "seed of the woman." The DNA of all humanity violates God's creative order that was established during creation.

"And God said, Let the earth bring forth grass, the herb yielding seed, and the fruit tree yielding fruit after his kind, whose seed is in itself, upon the earth: and it was so" (Genesis 1:11 KJB).

Looking at the tail end of this scripture and observing how it ends, it doesn't say it was good, but it ends by saying it was so. Could it be that in the world that existed in Genesis 1:1, the same violation occurred, which is why He never calls it good, the first angelic invasion.

"See also: Conflict of Adam and Eve with Satan, the Book of Enoch, the Enochic Book of Giants, and the Book of Jubilees refer to the Watchers, who are paralleled to the "sons of God" in Genesis 6 [30]." [13] Some consider the Epistle of Barnabas to acknowledge the Enochian version.

9

AS IN THE DAYS OF NOAH

"This is the account of Noah and his family. Noah was a righteous man, blameless among the people of his time, and he walked faithfully with God. Noah had three sons: Shem, Ham, and Japheth. Now the earth was corrupt in God's sight and was full of violence. God saw how corrupt the earth had become, for all the people on earth had corrupted their ways. So God said to Noah, I am going to put an end to all people, for the earth is filled with violence because of them. I am surely going to destroy both them and the earth. So make yourself an ark of cypress wood; make rooms in it and coat it with pitch inside and out" (Genesis 6:9-14 NIV).

"I am going to bring floodwaters on the earth to destroy all life under the heavens, every creature that has the breath of life in it. Everything on the earth will perish. But I will establish my covenant with you, and you will enter the ark, you and your sons and your wife and your sons' wives with you. You are to bring into the ark two of all living creatures, male and female, to keep them alive with you. Two of every kind of bird, of every kind of animal and of every kind of creature that moves along the ground will come to you to be kept alive. You are to take every kind of food that is to be eaten and store it away as food for you and them" (Genesis 6:17-21 NIV).

"The Lord then said to Noah, Go into the ark you and your whole family, because I have found you righteous in this generation. Of every clean beast thou shalt take thee by sevens, the male and his female. Fowl also of the air by sevens, the male and the female; to keep seed alive upon the face of all the earth" (Genesis 7:1-3 NIV).

God is trying to save all humanity and to preserve the "seed of the woman." It is essential to know that the whole genetic pool of humans and animals is compromised, except for Noah's family and the animals that Noah was instructed to preserve in the Ark, through the second angelic invasion.

Through the flood, God demonstrated His love and redemptive plan through His seed to all humanity. The Bible states that He "found Noah righteous in this generation." He is not implying that Noah and his family were sinless or morally perfect, but that their genetic chromosomes (DNA) are not contaminated by the abomination the "sons of God" had introduced to all creation.

In the book of Romans, Paul the Apostle tells us that we all have sinned: "For all have sinned and fall short of the glory of God" (Romans 3:23 NIV).

To understand the declaration that the Apostle Paul is making, "for all have sinned," we have to go back to the garden of Eden and look at Adam when he sinned and transgressed against God. Through him, we "all have sinned and fallen," so Noah was not without sin, but his family bloodline was not contaminated.

When we look at the flood and its narrative, God uses it to eradicate the earth of the abomination that the "sons of God" created.

The sin and evil upon the earth angered God to the extent that the only way He could preserve the "seed of the woman" was to destroy the earth.

"Then the Lord said, 'My Spirit will not contend with humans forever, for they are mortal; their days will be a hundred and twenty years'" (Genesis 6:3 NIV). God now makes a prophetic declaration concerning the destruction of the earth. He did not spare the ancient world when He brought the flood on its ungodly people, but protected Noah, a preacher of righteousness, and seven others.

Peter declares that "only eight people were spared in the ancient world" (2 Peter 2:5) because Noah was a righteous preacher. Throughout the Bible, it is very consistent that God found Noah to be a righteous man, but he was not without sin. The Bible tells us that the last days will be like the days of Noah. To understand the events and the earth's condition in the last days, we need to investigate and look further into the earth's state in "the days of Noah."

We know that in the beginning, after 4,000 years of living in obedience, Satan gets Adam and Eve to rebel against the instruction of God, and all the earth becomes evil and corrupt. "The Lord saw that the wickedness of man was great in the earth, and every intent of the thoughts of his heart was only evil continually" (Genesis 6:5 NKJV).

Because of this, God gave the generation of Noah and all of humanity 120 years to repent from evil, but as the "sons of God" continued to corrupt humanity's DNA, it became impossible to ignore the condition of all humanity.

"Although they knew God, they did not glorify Him as God, nor were thankful, but became futile in their thoughts, and their foolish hearts were darkened" (Romans 1:21 NKJV).

The Apostle Paul tells us that the days before the return of Christ will be like the days of Noah. "But mark this: There will be terrible times in the last days. People will be lovers of themselves, lovers of money, boastful, proud, abusive, disobedient to their parents, ungrateful, unholy, without love, unforgiving, slanderous, without self-control, brutal, not lovers of good, treacherous, rash, conceited, lovers of pleasure rather than lovers of God, having a form of godliness but denying its power. Have nothing to do with such people" (2 Timothy 3:1-5 NIV).

Because of governments, humans in the millions have been killed in wars, as per current statistics. "Roe v. Wade, 410 U.S. 113, was a landmark decision of the U.S. Supreme Court in which the Court ruled that the Constitution of the United States protects a pregnant woman's liberty to choose to have an abortion without excessive government restriction; date decided: January 22, 1973."[1]

Through abortion, the human race collectively and deliberately kills about 44 million innocent children a year (Global Abortion Rates, 2008).

"Accord to the 2011 Abortion Surveillance Report issued by the Center for Disease Control, black women make up 14 percent of childbearing population yet obtained 36.2 percent of abortions. Black women have the highest abortion ratio in the country, with 474 abortions per 1,000 live births. Percentage at these levels illustrate the more than 19 Million black babies have been aborted "Killed" since 1973."[2]

In the Bible, a Canaanite deity, "Molech," was associated with the practice of child sacrifice, what we have legalized and call Abortion in our society.

"They have also built the high places of Baal, to burn their sons with fire for burnt offerings unto Baal, which I commanded not, nor spoke it, neither came it into my mind" (Jeremiah 19:5 KJV).

In medieval and modern times, "Molech" is portrayed as a human hybrid having the head of a bull and the body of a human with his arms stretched out over the fire.

Once again, the Bible comments on cross breeding between humans and animals. This time, it is revealed through the Canaanite deity "Molech," a pagan god. Instead of worshiping "Yahweh," the Israelites chose to worship this pagan God and commit child sacrifice and the abuse of children. We are now living in a society where we have turned to pagan gods and legalized human sacrifice.

The world is changing rapidly, and we are truly living in the last days. "For out of the heart proceed evil thoughts, murders, adulteries, fornications, thefts, false witness, blasphemies" (Matthew 15:19 KJV).

Consider the Bohemian Club, "an elite invitation-only social club founded in San Francisco in 1872 by a group of male artists, writers, actors, lawyers, and journalists, all of means and interested in arts and culture. Since its founding, the club has expanded to include politicians and affluent business people.

The club is known primarily for its annual summer retreat at what is known as Bohemian Grove in the Redwood Forest of California's Sonoma County. Notable members over the years have included Clint Eastwood, Henry Kissinger, Walter Cronkite, Richard Nixon, Ronald Reagan, Charles Schwab, Ambrose Bierce, Bret Harte, Mark Twain, and Jack London.

The annual trip to Sonoma began in the summer of 1876. In the 20th century, the members' retreat garnered a reputation for involving highly secretive and cultish rituals, the most well known of which was the "Cremation of Care," instituted in 1881—an opening ceremony whose purpose was to make club members "carefree" from the outset of the retreat. That performance took place in front of the large concrete owl [type of Molech] (built 1929) in the center of the camp at Bohemian Grove." [3]

Could it be possible that the law of Roe v. Wade, 410 U.S. 113, landmark decision of the U.S. Supreme Court in which the Court ruled that the Constitution of the United States protects a pregnant woman's liberty to choose to have an abortion without excessive government restriction; was used with the intent to legally practice child sacrifice to "Molech," and call it Abortion in our society.

Humanity is rejecting the principles of God, has become very wicked in their ways, has hardened their hearts, and is now tampering with human genetics with the ideas of human evolution, "transhumanism," and "human hybrids."

In the twenty-first century, we hold it within our grasp to permanently alter the human race. We want to undo the current human DNA genetic code with robotics and nanotechnology.

If we look at history, this is what Adolf Hitler dreamed of. He wanted to create a superhuman race in his generation.

"Transhumanism is a philosophical movement, the proponents of which advocate and predict the enhancement of the human condition by developing and making widely available sophisticated technologies able to enhance longevity, mood, and cognitive abilities significantly.

Some transhumanism believes that human beings may eventually be able to transform themselves into beings with abilities so greatly expanded from the current condition as to merit the label of posthuman beings." [4]

Scientists are currently working on projects involving genetic technology to enhance the human species by making them more intelligent and robust, changing their physical appearance, and eliminating aging. Max Mehlman, a law professor, receives a grant of $773,000 to lead a team of low professors, physicians, and bioethicists in a two-year project.

They will develop guidelines and policies for humans to use as test subjects as we approach errors in genetic enhancement. Recently, a Canadian cloning group, the Raelians, declared their intent to begin cloning humans overseas.

The establishment of "safe havens" for genetic enhancement research poses several problems for countries that ban the submission of a DNA sample for rapid analysis. Under current law, customs officers can search people entering the country, even without a warrant or probable cause, as long as they reasonably suspect that the person may have committed an unlawful act.

In our current situation in the political realm, especially in the last year and a half because of the Coronavirus pandemic and our new leadership in government, we are starting to see a lot of laws implemented that are more liberal. With this current government, laws will be passed for transhumanism experiments. North Carolina is one of the top locations in the world for GMOs.

The United States is genetically engineering soybeans, field corn, cotton, and canola GMO crops. This trend also impacts the global community of genetically modifying organisms to promote agricultural innovation. Genetically Modified Organisms (GMOs) are a transgenic crop and use recombinant DNA technology to produce engineered crops.

This scientific modification in crops is possible because all organisms share the same DNA coding system, which can form strands of genes. This is how they can combine genetic material with unrelated organisms. Then there are the terms "human-animal hybrid" and "animal-human hybrid," which will incorporate an entity of elements from humans and animals to transport organs.

Human and animal hybrids terrorized humanity in the days of Noah. Now we have scientists committing the same abomination that the "sons of God" committed when they saw the "daughters of men" and took them as wives, giving birth to the Nephilim, and the earth was corrupt in God's sight and was full of violence.

God saw how corrupt the earth had become, for all the people on earth had corrupted their ways, and He decided to eradicate all flesh that had become corrupted.

There have been recent scientific advances regarding creating the "first human-pig hybrid embryos." The purpose of growing embryos, which are human, inside animals is to be used in transplants at the Salk Institute in California.

These human-animal hybrids are referred to as "chimeras" in Greek mythology. A hybrid of human and animal is unnatural in God's eyes and is also perceived as unnatural in biology.

"Our genes and DNA are shared across species, such that humans and mice share around 90% of their DNA, and we share around 35% of our genes with the simple roundworm." [5]

The scientific world is trying to justify human and animal experiments to prevent the loss of life by having organs available for transplants instead of relying on donated organs, and they are manufacturing replacement organs.

"Dr. Hiromitsu Nakauchi, at the University of Tokyo, and his team have successfully created a rat with a pancreas of mouse cells. The pancreas was later transplanted into a mouse engineered to have diabetes, and the mouse was effectively cured." [6]

The world as we know it is accelerating in the technological sphere. Transhumanism may be used for human enhancement—the possibility of extending life and increasing humanity's mental and physical abilities. The most recent advancement in the race towards Tranhumanism occurred when Elon Musk revealed the Neuralink "N1" BCI Device & The Path To Transhumanism without considering the theological concerns for the Christian community and the creation of an abomination in the eyes of God.

"But God gives it a body as he has determined, and to each kind of seed, he gives its own body. Not all flesh is the same: People have one kind of flesh, animals have another, birds another and fish another" (1 Corinthians 15:38-39 NIV). God makes it very clear that not all flesh is the same, and man was never meant to mix with other creatures, for all creatures have their flesh, and both have different spirits.

"Who knows if the human spirit rises upward and if the spirit of animals goes down to the earth?" (Ecclesiastes 3:21 NIV). God is explicitly telling us that the spirits of man go upward, and the spirits of animals go down into the earth because we are not the same. Only man has been created in the image of God, and the animal kingdom was created after their kind.

"So God created the great creatures of the sea and every living thing with which the water teems and that move about in it, according to their kinds, and every winged bird according to its kind. And God saw that it was good. God blessed them and said, 'Be fruitful and increase in number and fill the water in the seas, and let the birds increase on the earth'" (Genesis 1:21-22 NIV).

God, through the scripture, is directly concerning the mixture of flesh at the beginning of creation. He and His Word do not change, so His Word is still valid in the twenty-first century. There is to be no mixing of flesh, for "He created us in His likeness, so that we could rule over the fish in the sea and the birds in the sky, over the livestock and all the wild animals, and over all the creatures that move along the ground." This is the order that He created (Genesis 1:26 CSB).

When we look at the order of creation, He formed man and created the beasts of the field, for He "formed man out of dust and breathed the breath of God into man, and he became a living being" (Genesis 2:7 KJV).

We are living in the last days, as we are starting to see genetic contamination throughout the earth, as in the days of Noah. God put an end to the marriage of angels and humans and to the mixture of all flesh in the days of Noah. He will cleanse the earth with fire in the last days. At creation, He established order and maintained it even after the fall (Genesis. 8:22).

The absolute power of the Creator manifested in the continual working out of His plan for the world and His people in an orderly, contingent, and gracious way (Isaiah 45:11-25).

God's faithfulness, which comes from His lordship, guarantees that His absolute power is that of a good, benevolent Ruler who is coming to destroy the giants of this present day.

The giants of this present day, are both physical and spiritual, and they are hidden in our government, politicians, universities, and corporations, working under the demonic influence of Satan.

From a global perspective, the condition of the world has changed in recent years due to COVID-19. Look at the root cause of the pandemic— biopolitics is emerging alongside our global economic politics and cultural politics so that we can embrace transhumanism.

We live in an era where technology is enhancing the way we live and communicate; regardless of the effects on what's natural, our private and public institutions will continue to improve technologies that will change humanity's evolution into something that God did not create.

Democratic transhumanism will assert that humanity will be happier and more in control of their lives if they put their faith in science.

For most of these experiments, embryo use in research is increasing and will play an essential role in emerging biopolitics.

The emerging spectrum in biopolitics will start with the intellectuals and the activists. Satan is after "the seed," and through techno-utopianism and the left, they are trying to infiltrate the church. As the church, locally and globally, we must be firm on where we stand concerning transhumanism and human hybrids.

They want us to adapt to the belief in science because the evolutionistic humanities will progress. The left wants to use science to delegitimize the power of the church. "Techno-utopianism, atheism, and scientific rationalism have been associated with the democratic, revolutionary, and utopian left for most of the last two years"(Lambert M. Surhone, Miriam T. Timpledon, Susan F. Marseken VDM Publishing, May 19, 2010 - Technology & Engineering).

Radicals, feminists, racism, economics, and global pandemics have all been used to manipulate and control the end time.

"And Jesus answered him, Blessed are you, Simon Bar-Jonah! For flesh and blood has not revealed this to you, but my Father who is in heaven. And I tell you Peter, and on this rock I will build my Church, and the gates of hell shall not prevail against it. I will give you the keys of the kingdom of heaven, and whatever you bind on earth shall be bound in heaven, and whatever you loose on earth shall be loosed in heaven" (Mathew 16:17-19 NKJV).

As ministers of the Gospel of Jesus Christ, we must start teaching truth and empowering the church. For too many years, men have gotten rich off the Gospel and have been living a life of hypocrisy.

Within recent years, we have entered the season of the changing of the guards where God is starting to expose those who have been prostituting the Gospel. We will see an emergence of men and women who have a genuine heart for the Kingdom.

The emergence of philosophers, governments, liberals, and theologians as they confront these ethical issues in medicine and biological research is giving birth to the scientific evolution of the human species.

The church needs to grow up and prepare for the times and seasons coming against the Church. The church is in an apostate condition and must wake up and not conform to the new ideas of transhumanism, human-hybrids, and the philosophies of this world, as we are quickly racing to the culmination of the "end times."

10

THE GIANTS APPEAR AGAIN

"Then God blessed Noah and his sons and said to them, Have many children; grow in number and fill the earth. Every animal on earth, every bird in the sky, every animal that crawls on the ground, and every fish in the sea will respect and fear you. I have given them to you. Everything that moves, everything that is alive, is yours for food. Earlier I gave you the green plants, but now I give you everything for food. But you must not eat meat that still has blood in it, because blood gives life. I will demand blood for life. I will demand the life of any animal that kills a person, and I will demand the life of anyone who takes another person's life. Whoever kills a human being will be killed by a human being, because God made humans in his own image" (Genesis 9:1-6 NCV).

God makes a covenant with His creation, this time with Noah and his family, because out of his family are all the descendants of the earth and the "seed of the woman."

God uses Noah and his family to reverse the curse of the "sons of God" and the Nephilim because man had become very wicked. Satan's plan to corrupt the genetic DNA of all humanity was a total rebellion against God.

"But during this rebellion, Noah and his family find favor in the eyes of God" (Genesis 6:8). God chose Noah at the right time for this purpose because it is important to remember that God saw that generation's wickedness and corruption but preserved Noah and his family. Even though

God lavished His grace on Noah and his family, Noah was responsible for obeying his covenant with God.

The Creator of the universe was not responding to Noah's obedience or righteousness, but God found favor with Noah and chose him and his family to preserve His seed.

"Then Noah built an altar to the Lord and, taking some of all the clean animals and clean birds; he sacrificed burnt offerings on it" (Genesis 8:20 NIV).

God made a covenant with Noah that He would never destroy the earth with a flood but promises to preserve the earth. He told Noah and all of creation that His divine plan to redeem the earth would pass, and genetically pure humans would once again inhabit the earth.

What God intended from the beginning of time and what was started in Genesis in the Garden of Eden was to be sustained in the Noahic covenant. Satan, however, still had a plan. He was relentless in his pursuit of attacking Noah and his family. He sought to corrupt all of humanity by once again altering its DNA.

"And the sons of Noah, that went forth of the ark, were Shem, and Ham, and Japheth: and Ham is the father of Canaan. These are the three sons of Noah: and of them was the whole earth overspread. And Noah began to be a husbandman, and he planted a vineyard: And he drank of the wine, and was drunken; and he was uncovered within his tent. And Ham, the father of Canaan, saw the nakedness of his father, and told his two brethren without. And Shem and Japheth took a garment, and laid it upon both their shoulders, and went backward, and covered the nakedness of their father; and their faces were backward, and they saw not their father's nakedness. And Noah awoke from his wine, and knew what his younger son had done unto him. And he said, Cursed be Canaan; a servant of servants shall he be unto his brethren.

And he said, blessed be the Lord God of Shem; and Canaan shall be his servant. God shall enlarge Japheth, and he shall dwell in the tents of Shem; and Canaan shall be his servant" (Genesis 9:18-27 KJV).

The Bible tells us that after the flood, the giants appear again in the land of Canaan. There seems to be controversy among theologians and scholars on the assumption that the Nephilim returned after the flood.

"The first assumption is that the Nephilim after the flood must have descended from the Nephilim that existed before the flood." [1]

"Nephilim," used in Genesis 6:4, is the word *nephil* or *nephiyl* in Hebrew. When translated, it simply means "the fallen." In the first couple of chapters, I discussed why the Bible gives evidence that these were fallen angels, but the debate in question is how they appeared again.

"The Nephilim were on the earth in those days and also afterward, when the sons of God went to the daughters of humans and had children by them. They were the heroes of old, men of renown" (Genesis 6:4 NIV).

We know the Bible is clear that the Nephilim reappear, but the debatable assumption is how.

"The second assumption, which is highly debatable and holds no theological evidence, is that the Nephilim are understood to be regular humans and that there is no reason to assume that they all died." [2]

Through proper Biblical interpretation, we have already concluded that the Nephilim were not regular humans but were the offspring of the "sons of God" and the "daughters of men."

"The third assumption is that Og, one of these Nephilim, clung to Noah's ark and lived through the flood, but there is no Biblical evidence confirming this theory, and the Bible is clear in the book of Genesis that no one survived the flood." [3]

"The water rose and covered the mountains to a depth of more than fifteen cubits. Every living thing that moved on land perished, birds, livestock, wild animals, all the creatures that swam over the earth, and all humankind.

Everything on dry land with the breath of life in its nostrils died. Every living thing on the face of the earth was wiped out. People, animals, creatures that move along the ground, and birds were wiped from the earth. Only Noah was left, and those with him in the ark" (Genesis 7: 18-23 NIV).

The Bible tells us that Noah was "a righteous man, blameless among the people of his time, and he walked faithfully with God. Noah had three sons: Shem, Ham and Japheth" (Genesis 6:9 NIV).

But we also know that God allowed Noah to enter the ark "with his wife, and his sons' wives to keep the covenant that He had established with Noah" (Genesis 6:18).

The Bible does not indicate that the wives of Noah's sons were women with no trace of the Nephilim DNA, and the Bible clearly states that all the people of the earth had been corrupted, except Noah and his family.

Throughout Biblical history, the giants appear again in the land of Canaan, where Ham and his wife settled, and the Bible tells us Nimrod was a direct descendent of Ham.

"And the sons of Ham; Cush, and Mizraim, and Phut, and Canaan. And the sons of Cush; Seba, and Havilah, and Sabtah, and Raamah, and Sabtechah: and the sons of Raamah; Sheba, and Dedan. And Cush begat Nimrod; he began to be a mighty one in the earth. He was a mighty hunter before the Lord: Wherefore it is said, Even as Nimrod the mighty hunter before the Lord and the beginning of his kingdom was Babel, and Erech, and Accad, and Calneh, in the land of Shinar" (Genesis 10:6-10 KJV).

Nimrod, also known as Nemrod, is "the first of the earth to be a mighty man." When we look at the phrase "mighty man" in the Bible, it always refers to the Nephilim.

"The Nephilim were on the earth in those days, and also afterward, when the sons of God came in to the daughters of man and they bore children to them. These were the 'mighty men' who were of old, the men of renown" (Genesis 6:4).

We know that Canaan, the child of Ham, was the father of many giants who populated the nations in the Bible.

"And Canaan begat Sidon his first born, and Heth, And the Jebusite, and the Amorite, and the Girgasite, And the Hivite, and the Arkite, and the Sinite, And the Arvadite, and the Zemarite, and the Hamathite: and afterward were and the families of the Canaanites spread abroad. And the border of the Canaanites was from Sidon, as thou comest to Gerar, unto Gaza: as thou goest, unto Sodom, and Gomorrah, and Admah, and Zebiom, even unto Lasha. These are the sons of Ham, after their families, after their tongues, in their countries, and in their nations" (Genesis 10:15-20 KJV).

The Bible is very clear that through the lineage of Ham, the giants started to dominate the Promised Land, and once again, Satan was out to destroy "the seed of the woman" by infesting the nations with Nephilim DNA.

The flood had destroyed all the hybrid men and hybrid creatures. But Satan, in his relentless attack, was still trying to sabotage the birth of the Messiah.

The scene is set for one of the most intense battles in the history of humanity between two bloodlines, the "seed of the woman" and the "seed of the serpent." The Bible tells us that Satan strategically surrounded the Promised Land with giants. The tribes of giants that surrounded the Promised Land were the Amorites, the Emim, the Zamzummim, the Raphaim, the Nephilim, and the Anakim.

"In the fourteenth year, Kedorlaomer and the kings allied with him went out and defeated the Rephaites in Ashteroth Karnaim, the Zuzites in Ham, the Emites in Shaveh Kiriathaim, and the Horites in the hill country of Seir, as far as El Paran near the desert. Then they turned back and went to En Mishpat (that is, Kadesh), and they conquered the whole territory of the Amalekites, as well as the Amorites who were living in Hazezon Tamar" (Genesis 14:5-7 NIV).

It is evident that Satan planned to subdue the Promised Land, but in the midst of this rebellion, God separated a people through whom the "seed of the woman" would give birth to the Messiah. He chose Abraham, a descendent of Adam, and preserved the genealogies of the human race through a pure bloodline, that of Enoch, Noah, and Shem, that ultimately produced a Holy Seed that would redeem humanity to the image of God.

"Now the Lord had said unto Abram, Get thee out of thy country, and from thy kindred, and from thy father's house, unto a land that I will shew thee: And I will make of thee a great nation, and I will bless thee, and make thy name great; and thou shalt be a blessing: And I will bless them that bless thee, and curse him that curseth thee: and in thee shall all families of the earth be blessed" (Genesis 12: 1-3 KJV).

God's chosen people and nation would bring forth the "seed" to redeem a fallen race. In Abraham's journey to bring forth the "seed," he had to face and conquer a land infested with the Nephilim.

As Abraham listened to the voice and promises of God, there was a prophetic utterance in his spirit, soul, and mind that echoes through the history of time. It is the manifestation of the "seed of the woman" that would usher in the seed of Abraham. "That in blessing I will bless thee, and in multiplying I will multiply thy seed as the stars of heaven, and as the sand which is upon the seashore; and thy seed shall possess the gate of his enemies" (Genesis 22:17 KJV).

"And Abram passed through the land unto the place of Sichem, unto the plain of Moreh. And the Canaanite was in the land. And the Lord appeared unto Abram, and said, Unto thy seed will I give this land and there builded he an alter unto the Lord, who appeared unto him" (Genesis 12:6-7 KJV).

The covenant made between the Creator of the universe and Abram said that he would be the father of many nations and that his bloodline would produce kings.

God chose Abraham to be the father of Israel and all the nations of the earth. We know that Abraham's name was originally Abram, but to bless him and make a great nation, God changed his name.

Why is it suggested that Abram means, "exalted father" and Abraham means the "father of multitudes" or "the father of many nations"? Both mean the same thing: "exalted father." In the book of Genesis, we see that God makes a promise to Abram: "I will make you into a great nation, and I will bless you; I will make your name great, and you will be a blessing" (Genesis 12:2 NIV).

Abraham obeys God's call upon his life, leaves the land of his birthplace, Mesopotamia, and travels to the land of Canaan with his wife Sarah, his nephew Lot, and all of their possessions (Genesis 12:1-6).

As prophetic people, we know that whenever God gives a prophetic word, that word will be tried and tested. This was no different for Abraham, as he had to put his faith in the God he served because Satan took another opportunity to corrupt the DNA of the bloodline of the One who would redeem creation.

"And there was famine in the land: and Abram went down into Egypt to sojourn there; for the famine was grievous in the land. And it came to pass, when he was come near to enter into Egypt, which he said unto Sarai his wife, Behold now, I know that thou art a fair woman to look upon: Therefore is shall come to pass, when the Egyptians shall see thee, that they shall say, This is his wife: and they will kill me, but they will save thee alive. Say, I pray thee, thou art my sister: that it may be well with me for thy sake; and my soul shall live because of thee. And it came to pass, that when Abram was come into Egypt, the Egyptians beheld the woman that she was fair. The princes also of Pharaoh saw her, and commended her before Pharaoh: and the woman was taken into Pharaoh's house. And he entreated Abram well for her sake: and he had sheep, and oxen, and he asses, menservants, and maidservants, and she asses, and camels" (Genesis 12:10-16 KJV).

The Bible tells us that because of Abraham's choice to deceive Pharaoh by telling him that Sarah was his sister, he jeopardizes the plan of redemption for the entire world. Then there is the nephew of Abraham, Lot, who is always displaying poor judgment when it comes to his family. These flaws in his character result in the act of incest by the daughters of Lot.

"And Lot went up out of Zoar, and dwelt in the mountain, and his two daughters with him; for he feared to dwell in Zoar: and he dwelt in a cave, he and his two daughters. And the firstborn said unto the younger, Our father is old, and there is not a man in the earth to come in unto us after the manner of all the earth: Come, let us make our father drink wine, and we will lie with him, that we may preserve the seed of our father. And they made their father drink wine that night: and the firstborn went in, and lay with her father, and he perceived not when she lay down, nor when she arose. And it came to pass on the morrow, that the firstborn said unto the younger, Behold, I lay yesterday night with my father: let us make him drink wine this night also; and go thou in, and lie with him, that we may preserve the seed of our father. And they made their father drink wine that night also: and the younger arose, and lay with him; and he perceived not when she lay down, nor when she arose. Thus were both daughters of Lot with child by their father. And the firstborn bare a son, and called his mane Moab: and the same is the father of the Moabites unto this day. And the younger; she also bare a son, and called his name Benammi: the same is the father of the children of Ammon unto this day" (Genesis 19:30-38 KJV).

Throughout Biblical history, the seed of Lot and his daughters resulted in the birth of the Moabite and Amorite nations, who fought with the Israelites over territory and worshiped pagan gods, Chemosh and Molech.

The Amorite god Molech was a god of infant sacrifice: "And you shall not let any of your descendants pass through the fire to Molech, nor shall you profane the mane of your God I am the Lord" (Leviticus 18:21 NKJV).

The Moabite god Chemosh had a thirst for blood sacrifice, and we find that human sacrifice was part of their rites: "Then he took his eldest son that should have reigned in his stead and offered him for a burnt offering upon the wall. And there was great wrath against Israel: and they departed from him, and returned to their land" (2 Kings 3:27 KJV).

Through the bloodline of Lot and his daughter and the inhabitants of Sodom and Gomorrah, they create a people threatening the bloodline of the Messiah, for they were wicked people.

Satan continued to wage war against the "seed of the woman," but God is a covenant-keeping God and promised to make a great nation of Abraham, saying He would bless him and his seed, and his name would be great (Genesis 12:2).

"And the Lord said unto Abram; after Lot was separated from him, Lift up now thine eyes, and look from the place where thou art northward, and southward, and eastward, and westward: For all the land which thou seest, to thee will I give it, and to thy seed for ever. And I will make thy seed as the dust of the earth, then shall thy seed also be numbered. Arise; walk through the land in the length of it and in the breadth of it; for I will give it unto thee. Then Abram removed his tent, and came and dwelt in the plain of Mamre, which is Hebron, and built there an altar unto the Lord" (Genesis 13:14-18 KJV).

The Bible states that Abraham and Sarah had still not given birth to their promised child, but we know that Abraham was still carrying the seed that would redeem all of creation.

The Bible makes it clear that the Nephilim and the giants produced through Ham's bloodline have always been the main threat against the "seed of the woman," even after the deluge and dwelling in the land of Sodom and Gomorrah.

We know that with all the attempts to destroy the "seed of the woman," the Bible tells us of Mary, "she was found to be pregnant through the Holy Spirit" (Matthew 1:18).

She gives birth to the Messiah, Jesus, who was crucified to redeem a fallen creation (Matthew 27:32-56).

11

THE BLOODLINE OF THE NEPHILIM

Nephilim, half-angelic and half-human hybrids, the by-product of fallen angels and human women who were given to each other in an illicit marriage from Adam to the days of Noah. The Nephilim returned after the days of Noah and settled throughout the Promised Land and in the ancient Middle East.

Throughout the Bible, it is evident that they were one of the primary enemies of God and His chosen nation, Israel. As we continue to explore the bloodline of the Nephilim, we will see that they genetically altered all flesh, both the human species and the animal kingdom.

"So the Lord said, 'I will wipe from the face of the earth the human race I have created and with them all the animals, the birds and the creatures that move along the ground, for I regret that I have made them'" (Genesis 6:7 NIV).

The earth was biologically altered, and the only way to save the human race was to destroy all the creations that were genetically different from what God had created. Now they were no longer lovers of God but were worshiping Satan and his angels.

"Now the earth was corrupt in God's sight and was full of violence. God saw how corrupt the earth had become, for all the people on earth had corrupted their ways" (Genesis 6:11-12 NIV).

The Bible makes it very clear that the "sons of God" took human women and had sex with them, corrupting all of humanity and the animal kingdom.

Christianity is based on God's Word being established and revealed through the Bible, but the church has not preached or spoken much about the Nephilim.

Your worldview will change in the present age concerning past and current events related to the Bible and our relationship with God as the universal church of God, "the body of Christ," learns more about this Nuclear Atomic weapon released on the earth in the days of Noah. A clear understanding is that these events did happen and that the fight for the survival of the human race is real. This fight is still very much alive today in the twenty-first century.

The Bible makes it very clear that angels were having sexual relationships with human women. The beings who were born with this genetically corrupted seed were Satanic-created superhumans.

These superhumans dominated the world with violence; these are the "men of renown." These men were famous and legendary; they were looked upon as gods, titans, and "demigods," and these are the myths spoken about in Greek mythology.

"There were giants in the earth in those days; and also after that, when the sons of God came in unto the daughters of men and they bare children to them, the same became mighty men which were of old, men of renown" (Genesis 6:4 NKJV).

As we look at the origin of the gods of Greek mythology and the "men of renown" in the book of Genesis, we will discover that they are one and the same. The Jews and scholars of old and Christians in the twenty-first century that don't study Scripture would never admit that they were one and the same, but as we look at the works of Titus Flavius Josephus, it is evident that they were.

In Greek mythology, the Greek gods are the Nephilim, which means "fallen ones," and their fathers are the "sons of God." The ancient Greeks also believe that they were destroyed by a massive flood like the accounts of Genesis.

In Greek mythology, "Zeus, the king of the gods, resolved to destroy all humanity by a flood. Deucalion was warned by his father, the God Prometheus, of the imminent doom and constructed an ark in which, according to one version, he and his wife rode out the flood and landed on Mount Parnassus. The flood lasted nine days, and the couple were the only two surviving humans." [1] This story resembles the Biblical accounts of Noah's ark.

The ironic thing about both stories is that they need to eradicate a world that has become genetically contaminated with foreign DNA that has corrupted all creation. The earth needed to be purified through a flood and make humankind extinct.

Those saved through an ark were chosen because they were not genetically contaminated by celestial beings but were chosen to populate the earth again.

The only two people that are saved are "Deucalion," the son of Prometheus, known for his righteous character and sound advice, and his wife, Pyrrha, a very fair lady.

"The gods perceived them to be the most righteous amongst the men and women on Earth and had chosen them to be the only survivors of that catastrophe that was about to befall every man and animal." [2]

Once again, the accounts of Noah's family state that they were righteous, not meaning that they were not sinless, but genetically pure. Studying cultures worldwide, we will see that they all have a story or an account of a flood, and many of them refer to giants before the flood, as in the days of Noah.

Scholars and theologians are receiving illumination on the accounts of creation. Their worldview is starting to change, and they are more open to the actual accounts from Adam and Eve to Noah and the start of civilization after the flood, and the apocryphal writings and the book of Enoch but not held in the same authority as the Bible.

As we look into the Biblical narrative and what it reveals about the Nephilim, it states, "The last days shall be like the days of Noah."

"But of that day and hour knoweth that no man, no, not the angels of heavens but my Father only. But as the days of Noah were, so shall also the coming of the Son of Man be" (Matthew 24:36-37 KJV).

The Bible states that the last days shall be "as the days of Noah," and I believe we will see a new incursion of the Nephilim and hybrid humans.

The Bible and the Book of Enoch warned creation that the world would be destroyed because of these "fallen angels." God is warning His church by unveiling some truths and revealing the mystery that "the last days shall be like the days of Noah."

Christians have refused to accept some of the accounts of the Bible because they don't fit their paradigm, and as God's Word is fulfilled in these last days, they will start to question the validity of the Scriptures.

You may be asking for proof of the existence of these giants other than the Bible. The Book of Enoch and the Dead Sea Scrolls seem to be unreliable sources among many scholars, believers, and Gospel ministers.

The ancient cultures of our civilization were very advanced and diverse in science, astronomy, physics, and engineering. We now know through the Book of Enoch that the angels taught the early humans these secrets as they took human women for their wives.

"We know that the Greek Titans were partly terrestrial and partly celestial, rebelled against their father Uranus and, after a prolonged contest, were defeated by Zeus and condemned into Tartarus. They embody what the Bible describes as these hybrid creatures, Nephilim."[3]

In Greek mythology, Atlas and Hercules would be what the Book of Genesis refers to as the Nephilim. Legends of these human hybrids can be traced in the cultures of the American Indians, the South Sea Islands, the Mayans, the Incas, Bolivia, India, Greece, Persia, Gilgamesh, Egypt, Assyria, and Sumer. The one thing they all have in common are these star people, "sons of God," who cohabitated with human women and created a hybrid race of giants, the Nephilim.

A hybrid is an offspring of two different entities of different subspecies, a crossbreeding of two diverse entities that differ in their inheritable characteristics.

"Now it came to pass when men began to multiply on the face of the earth, and daughters were born to them, that the sons of God (angels) saw the daughters of men, that they were beautiful; they took wives for themselves of all whom they chose… There were giants (Nephilim) on the earth in those days and afterward, when the sons of God came into the daughters of men and they bore children to them. Those were the heroes of old, men of renown" (Genesis 6:1-2,4 NKJV).

The Bible makes a powerful declaration that something happened in humanity that was not normal but out of the natural structure God had ordained. The Bible and its authors are adamant in making sure that they validate this statement; the book of Jude states, "You also know that the angels who did not keep within their proper domain but abandoned their place of residence, he has kept in eternal chains in utter darkness locked up for the judgment of the great day. Sodom and Gomorrah and neighboring towns, since they indulged in sexual immorality and pursued unnatural desire in a way similar to these angels, are now displayed as an example of suffering the punishment of eternal fire" (Jude 1:6-7 NET).

He makes it clear that the "sons of God" left their habitation, had sexual relations with the daughters of men, and produced these famous hybrid "giants."

In the book of Genesis, God declares, "In the beginning, God created the heavens and the earth" (Genesis 1:1 KJV).

In this statement, God states that He created the heavens, "the solar system," and the earth. As we take a closer look at the solar system, we know that He created 11 planets, eight major and three minor planets. Going a little deeper into this statement in Genesis 4, "These offspring produced are famous, and you know of them and their existence," I want to declare that their names have forever been written in our solar system.

As we look at Mercury, the closest planet to the sun, it is named after the Roman god Mercurius, "Mercury," god of commerce, a messenger of the gods and mediator between the gods and the mortals, a Nephilim.

The second planet is Venus; it's the hottest planet and is the only planet to spin in the opposite direction of the Earth. And yet it is very close to the Earth; she gets her name from the "Roman goddess, whose functions encompassed love, beauty, desire, sex, fertility, prosperity, and victory," and she was a Nephilim (Venus the Goddess of Love).

The third planet is Mars, called "the Red Planet." Mars is the fourth planet from the sun and the second-smallest planet in the solar system, larger than only Mercury. In English, Mars carries the name of the Roman god of war. He is the son of Zeus and Hera, who had twins, Phobos and Deimos, named after two moons, according to Greek mythology.[4] He is considered the father of Romulus and Remus, the mystical twins, and he is also a Nephilim.

The fourth planet is the "dwarf planet Ceres," the largest object in the asteroid belt between Mars and Jupiter.[5]

THE ORIGIN OF SIN

In Greek mythology, "Ceres was the Roman goddess of agriculture, she was the goddess of the harvest and created to teach agriculture." She was the wife of Zeus and the daughter of Cronus and Rhea, and she is a Nephilim.[6]

The fifth planet, Jupiter, the largest in the solar system, is named after the Roman god Jupiter, who is the king of the gods in Roman mythology. He had two siblings: his brother Pluto and his sister Ceres.

"With the help of the cyclops and the giants, they declared war on Saturn and the other Titans."[7] After defeating the Titans, they are imprisoned in Tartarus, and he was also a Nephilim. He is also known as the god of the sky and thunderbolt.

The sixth planet is Saturn, and there is a hexagon on its north pole that is not a naturally occurring shape in nature. The hexagon maintains its shape while rotating, which is still an unexplainable phenomenon. Isn't it ironic that 666 is the Mark of the Beast, and the hexagon is also a sign of the devil and is used in witchcraft and Satanic cults? Saturn originates from the betrayer of his father, Uranus; this resembles the betrayal of Satan, "Lucifer," the one who betrays God.

The seventh planet is Uranus, the first planet discovered by William Herschel in 1781. It is the seventh planet from the sun, and its name refers to the Greek god of the sky, "Uranus," who, according to Greek mythology, was the great-grandfather of Ares, the grandfather of Zeus, and father of Cronus, the first ruler of the universe.

The eighth and last planet is Neptune, the "Ice Giant," the "farthest known solar planet from the sun in the solar system and the densest 'giant' planet. It is seventeen times the mass of the earth and slightly more massive than its near-twin Uranus."[8]

"The ice plant Neptune was the first planet located through mathematical calculations, using predictions made by Urbain Le Verrier, and Johann Galle discovered the planet in 1846. The planet is named after the Roman god of the sea, 'Poseidon,' a Nephilim."[9]

"Pluto is a dwarf planet in the Kuiper Belt, a ring of bodies beyond the orbit of Neptune, and it was the first and the largest Kuiper Belt object discovered in 1930. It was declared to be the ninth planet from the sun." Pluto, or "Hades," is the God of the Underworld, which is "Hell," and he can be better characterized as a demon. [10]

"Charon is the largest moon of the dwarf planet Pluto. James W. Christy and Robert S. Harrington at the U.S. Naval Observatory station in Flagstaff, Arizona discovered it telescopically in 1978. The moon was named for Charon, the ferryman of dead souls to the realm of Hades, the Greek counterpart of the Roman god Pluto in Greek mythology." [11] Charon is the ferryman who carries wicked souls across the River Styx to Hell; he is a Nephilim, or it can be said that he is a demon in the twenty-first century.

"Eris is the most massive and second-largest known dwarf planet in the solar system. In Greek mythology, Eris is the goddess of Strife or Discordia and the daughter of Dysnomia, which means lawlessness, a Nephilim. Never was there a more appropriately named body in the solar system. Astronomer Mike Brown of Caltech and his team discovered Eris in 2005."

Greek mythology and the Nephilim are influencing our world and the spiritual world, for nine of the eleven planets in our solar system have been named after Nephilim. Is this a coincidence, or is there something happening behind the scenes in the spiritual realm?

If we look at the days of the week, we will find that hidden in them are the names of the gods. Sunday is "Sun Day," Monday is "Moon Day," and Tuesday is "Twi's Day" or "Mars Day," who is the god of war; this is the Norse version, named after a Nephilim.

Thursdays are "Thor's Day" or "Jupiter Day," the god of thunderbolts. Then we have Wednesday, "Woden's Day" or "Mercury Day," the god of the Underworld, named after a Nephilim. Also name after a Nephilim is Friday, "Frigg's Day" or "Venus Day," the goddess of love. Saturday is "Saturn's Day," "Satan's Day," or "Sabbath Day" to God and is also named after a Nephilim.

As we look at our solar system, days of the week, and now months of the year, we will discover that the Nephilim "giants" have forever been embedded into our culture and society.

"January, as we know, is the first month of the year and contains 31 days. The term originated before the year 1000 from Middle English, ultimately deriving from the Latin noun use of Januarius to Janu(s) of Janus. In ancient Roman culture, Janus was a god of doorways, beginnings, and the rising and setting of the sun. His name comes from the Latin Janus, meaning "door, doorway, or entrance."

There were many gateways in Rome where ceremonial entrances and exits were made, especially for the army's departure on an expedition. As the god of transitions, Janus is often depicted with two bearded heads facing opposite directions, looking to both the future and the past; the two-faced god of gates" and a Nephilim.[12]

"February is named after an ancient Roman festival of purification called Februa, during a time when people were ritually washed." In this case, God was named after a festival, not a Nephilim/demon.[13]

"March is named after Mars, the Roman god of war. The Roman calendar began in March, and the months of January and February were added later, after a calendar reform." Identity: a Nephilim.

"April is named after the Greek goddess of love, Aphrodite. In the Roman calendar, the fourth month, April, is spelled Aprilis, meaning 'to open.'" Festivals planned for April included Parrilla, a day celebrating the founding of Rome; since Romans named some of the months after gods to honor their divinities, April is equivalent to the Greek goddess Aphrodite, and she is a Nephilim.[14]

"May named after Maia, she is the eldest of the Pleiades, the mother of Hermes, fathered by Zeus, and the daughter of Atlas; he was a Titan responsible for bearing the weight of the heavens on his shoulders."[15]

She was known as the nurturer of the earth and the growing surrounding planets. Her "Roman equivalent, Bona Dea, was known as the goddess of fertility and is associated with growth and springtime." She is a Nephilim.

"June is named after the Roman goddess Juno, the wife of Jupiter, queen of the gods, and the goddess of marriage. It is the sixth month of the year in the Julian and Gregorian calendars. Juno, the Roman goddess of youth and protection, her name in Latin, 'Iuno,' comes from the root word for young' (Iuuen) and goes back to the idea of viral energy and fertility," and she is a Nephilim.[16]

"July is the seventh month of the year (between June and August) in the Julian and Gregorian calendars and the fourth of seven months for a length of 31 days. The Roman Senate named it in honor of Roman general Julius Caesar in 44 BC. It was called the Quintilis, the fifth month of the 10-month calendar," and it gets its name from a Nephilim.[17]

Six of the twelve months of the year have been named after Nephilim; our society and culture are so embedded in the worship of these gods, and they are so much a part of our lives that they have become the norm.

"For we wrestle not against flesh and blood, but against principalities, against powers, against rulers of the darkness of this world, against spiritual wickedness in heavenly or 'high places'" (Ephesians 6:12 KJV).

"By the heavens is meant the space above our earth—namely the atmosphere; for in Scripture, we read three heavens; the first heaven is the open space above the earth, and above which the clouds roll, charged with the vapors from which the rain descends.

The second heaven is the higher space. Where the Sun, moon, and stars resolve. The third heaven is the place of the blessed. Paul tells us he was caught up to the 'third heaven.'"[18] It's evident through Scripture and science that the powers of the air rule in the second heaven.

Christians have been conditioned and taught that there is only one God, but the Bible clearly states that there are many gods. The one true God is "YHWH," the Alpha and Omega, the Beginning and the End.

The book of Exodus and the Exodus begin in a region called Goshen in the Egyptian region. Most early Jewish traditions acquaint Moses as the author of the book of Exodus because of the education provided to him in the royal courts of Egypt.

God entrusted Moses to fulfill His promise to Abraham, Isaac, and Jacob. In Exodus 12:12 the Bible states, "For I will pass through the land of Egypt that night, and I will strike all the firstborn in the land of Egypt, both man and beast; and on all the gods of Egypt I will execute judgment: I am the Lord."

Most of what has been taught in our churches is erroneous because we have been conditioned to believe that every supernatural battle we face is the devil. The devil is not omnipresent, so it's impossible for the condition of the world we live in and the spiritual warfare we encounter to be acquainted with the devil.

The Bible tells us, "For we do not wrestle against flesh and blood, but principalities, against powers, against the ruler of the darkness of this age, against spiritual hosts of wickedness in the heavenly places" (Ephesians 6:12 KJV).

The Bible makes it very clear that there are fallen angels, demons, or gods that have been wreaking havoc on planet Earth, setting the stage for a one-world government, the Antichrist, and the final war, Armageddon.

We are in the third week that Russia ("the bear") has invaded Ukraine as the world watches innocent women and children be killed. We are now in March of 2022, and the Bear and the Dragon have been poking their heads out. They are manipulating Russian President Vladimir Vladimirovich Putin to attack Ukraine and take control so that they can gain access to the Black Sea. They will strategically advance their naval ships to take control of the region and then advance into Jerusalem and Amman, located in the West Bank, where the final war will be fought, Armageddon.

"And behold, another beast, a second one, resembling a bear. And it was raised up on one side, and three ribs were in its mouth between its teeth; and thus they said to it, Arise, devour much meat" (Daniel 7:5 NASB).

The bear is on the move with the invasion of Ukraine. When we look at the bear's characteristics and study nature, especially when hungry or robbed and deprived of its young, the bear is known to be one of the most ferocious, fearless animals in a time of war, especially when provoked.

The Russian president is adamant that the breakup of the Soviet Union has deprived him of his young, and he seeks to reestablish the Soviet Union in his pursuit of fulfilling Biblical prophecy as the demonic spirits of the Nephilim seek to advance their plans as we advance to the culmination of Armageddon.

The book of Ezekiel, a prophet and priest of ancient Israel, gives us some insight into world events that occur in the last days: "Now the word of the Lord came to me, saying, Son of man, set your face against Gog, of the land of Magog, the prince of Rosh, Meshech, and Tubal, and prophesy against him, and say, Thus say the Lord God, I am against you, O Gog, the prince of Rosh, Meshech, and Tubal. I will turn you around, put hooks into your jaws, and lead you out, splendidly clothed with all your army, horses, and horsemen, a great company with bucklers and shields handling swords. Persia, Ethiopia, and Libya are with them, all with shields and helmets; Gomer and all its troops; the house of Togarmah from the far North, all its troops-many people are with you" (Ezekiel 38:1-6 NKJV).

Many wonder if Russia attacking Ukraine plays any part in these events, and the Bible shows that it does. When the Bible speaks about "Gog and Magog," it is talking about a leader in the land of Russia. "Gog and Magog" from the north in the twenty-first century is unequivocally Russia.

The book of Genesis has keys that unlock many mysteries throughout the Bible; the book of Genesis also reveals to us that Magog, Meshech, and Tubal were all sons of Japheth, who was one of the three sons of Noah.

The Bible tells us that Japheth and his family migrated to the area of modern-day Russia: "This is the accounts of Shem, Ham, and Japheth, Noah's sons, who themselves had sons after the flood. The Japhethites. The sons of Japheth; Gomer, Magog, Madai, Javan Tubai, Meshek and Tiras" (Genesis 10:1-2 NIV).

Moses, the author of the book of Genesis, had a clear prophetic understanding of the times and seasons of the end times and was able to write with the knowledge that Magog, Tubal, and Meshech would settle in the far north of Europe and eventually become the Russian population to fulfill the Biblical prophecy of the end times.

"For I will gather all the nations against Jerusalem to battle, and the city shall be taken and the houses plundered and the women raped, Half of the city shall not be cut off form the city, Then the Lord will go out and fight against those nations as when he fights on a day of battle. On that day his feet shall stand on the Mount of Olives that lies before Jerusalem on the east, and the Mount of Olives shall be split in two from east to west by a very side valley, so that one half of the Mount shall move northward, and the other half southward. And you shall flee to the valley of my mountains, for the valley of the mountains shall reach to Azal. And you shall flee as you fled from the earthquake in the days of Uzziah king of Judah. Then the Lord my God will come, and all the holy ones with him" (Zechariah 14:2-5 ESV).

Zechariah also gives us a prophecy of the end times as the demonic powers and principalities are preparing to "gather the nations"--Russia, the Middle East, the Arab-African coalition, and China—against Jerusalem for the final battle, Armageddon.

12

NIMROD AND THE TOWER OF BABEL

The Bible tells us that Nimrod was a mighty warrior who was the son of Cush and the great-grandson of Noah: "The sons of Ham: Cush, Egypt, Put and Canaan. The sons of Cush: Seba, Havilah, Sabtah, Raamah and Sabteka. The sons of Raamah: Sheba and Dedan" (Genesis 10:6-7 NIV).

Cush was the father [c] of Nimrod, who became a mighty warrior on the earth. He was a mighty hunter before the Lord; that is why it is said, "Like Nimrod, a mighty hunter before the Lord." The first centers of his kingdom were Babylon, Uruk, Akkad, and Kalneh, in [d] Shinar. [e] From that land he went to Assyria, where he built Nineveh, Rehoboth Ir, [f] Calah and Resen, which is Nineveh and Calah—which is the great city (Genesis 10:6-12).[1]

Through the lineage of Ham, we know the Nephilim DNA regenerated through the wife of Ham, and this passage in Genesis gives particular reference to Nimrod. Is there any Biblical proof that Nimrod was a giant, and we know through the line of Ham the Nephilim DNA is evident in his anatomy, or did he become a giant through a curse? We will look at the Septuagint and the Masoretic Text because they occasionally present a notable difference in translation, which is what some Biblical scholars have uncovered. They also explain why it was so crucial for Nimrod to erect the Tower of Babel.

The Book of Jubilees and the Book of Jasher also share essential information on uncovering the mysteries of Nimrod and the Tower of Babel. We know three interconnected passages exist through the statement "the mighty men of renown" in the Hebrew Bible. The first of the three statements in the Septuagint, or the Old Testament, was created for the Greek-speaking Jews in Egypt in the second.

The first occurrence is in Genesis: "When human beings began to increase in number on the earth and daughters were born to them, and sons of God saw that the daughters of humans were beautiful, and they married any of them they chose. Then the Lord said, 'My Spirit will not contend with humans forever, for they are mortal; their days will be a hundred and twenty years.' The Nephilim were on the earth in those days and afterward when the sons of God went to the daughters of humans and had children by them. They were the heroes of old, men of renown" (Genesis 6:1-4 NIV).

The second is found in the book of Numbers when Moses, the author, says, "They came back to Moses and Aaron and the whole Israelite community at Kadesh in the Desert of Paran. There, they reported to them and the whole assembly and showed them the fruit of the land. They gave Moses this account: 'We went into the land to which you sent us, and it does flow with milk and honey! Here is its fruit. But the people there are powerful, and the cities are fortified and large. We even saw descendants of Anak there. The Amalekites live in the Negev; the Hittites, Jebusites and the Amorites live in the hill country; and the Canaanites live near the sea and along the Jordan'" (Numbers 13:27-29 NIV).

The third found outside the Pentateuch in the book of Ezekiel. The prophet Ezekiel, the author of the book of Ezekiel, tells us: "But they do not lie with the fallen warriors of old, who went down to the realm of the dead with their weapons of war-their swords placed under their heads and their shields resting on their bones-though these warriors also terrorized the land of the living" (Ezekiel 32:27 NIV).

When we look at the phrases "fallen warriors of old" or "fallen Gibborim" as Gibborim Nephilim or Warriors Nephilim, in reference to the Nephilim in Genesis 6:4, then, as understood by Handel, the verse reads, "They lie with the warriors, the Nephilim of old, who descended to Sheol with their weapons of war. They placed their swords beneath their heads and their shields upon their bones, for the terror of the warriors was upon the land of the living" (Handel Roberts S. (1987). Of demigods and the deluge: Towards an interpretation of Genesis 6:1-4 NIV).

The "fallen Gibborim" is a Hebrew word classified as "mightiest," used many times to refer to men, lion hunters, soldiers, and leaders. So when we look further into the origin of the word "Gibborim," as in the book of Samuel, we are presented with two views: Nimrod was a human who processed superhuman strength, or he was a Nephilim.

"These be the names of the mighty men [gibborim] whom David had: The Tachmonite that sat in the seat, chief among the captains; the same was using the Ezmite: he lift up his spear against eight hundred, whom he slew at one time" (2 Samuel 23:8).

"Thus the word [Gibborim], relating principally to creatures possessed of power far superior to human might, is capable of being applied either to good or evil beings. Hence Nimrod is called a Gibbor or a giant, and by the same title, the Antichrist is addressed…"[2] The Septuagint states, "And [Cush] begot [Nimrod]: he began to be a mighty one or (giant) upon the earth, he was a mighty hunter or (giant) before the Lord God; therefore they say, As [Nimrod] the mighty hunter or (giant) before the Lord" (Genesis 10:8,9).

Scripture is unambiguous that Nimrod was not born mighty, but "he began to be a mighty one or giant," and now there's proof through the Book of Jasher that Nimrod was a giant. We know through the line of Ham that the Nephilim DNA is evident in his anatomy.

We know that "When human beings began to increase in number in the earth and daughters were born to them, the sons of God saw that the daughters of humans were beautiful, and they married any of them they chose" (Genesis 6:1-2).

As the "sons of God" married the daughters of Adam, they had children, and the by-product of this abomination altered the DNA of God's creation. These children (a new species) were called the Nephilim, "the mighty men who were of old, the men of renown." Because of the outright assault on humanity, Nimrod has Nephilim DNA in his anatomy that remained dormant until he was twenty years old.

What is the human genome? The human genome is the entire set of nucleic acid and sequences for humans, obtained by the Human Genome Project and completed in April 2003. It provides the first holistic view of our genetic heritage.

The 46 human chromosomes (22 pairs of autosomal and two sex chromosomes) between them house almost 3 billion base pairs of DNA, containing about 20,500 protein-coding genes.

The coding regions make up less than 5% of the genome (the function of all the remaining DNA is unclear), and some chromosomes have a higher density of genes than others." [3]

Four genetic disorders are inherited: single gene inheritance, multifactorial inheritance, chromosome abnormalities, and mitochondrial inheritance. When studied in detail, you will find that they cause or influence different disorders and diseases within the human body. Scientists have found that "Sometimes genes change due to issues within the DNA (mutation)."

"This can raise your risk of having a genetic disorder. Some cause symptoms at birth while others develop over time." [4]

When we look at "heredity genetics," we will find that many mental illnesses run in families, suggesting that they may be passed on from parents to children through genes.

We know that a person can inherit a susceptibility to a mental disorder, but this doesn't mean the person will develop the condition. Sometimes there are other factors called triggers, such as a psychological trauma, that can influence the change in a person with inherited genetics.

Through scientific research, we know that young adults ages 18 through 29 are in a stage where they are still experiencing cognitive development. At this age, psychological trauma can cause a trigger and change their inherited genetics.

With the knowledge that we have gained in the twenty-first century through inherited genetics/DNA, we know that "Cush had begotten Nimrod, he gave him those garments through his love for him, and Nimrod grew up, and when he was twenty years old, he put on those garments" (Jasher 7:29).

The Septuagint is clear that Nimrod "began to be a mighty one or giant" in those days. And we know through the Book of Jasher that Nimrod inherited genetics/DNA, experiencing trauma that caused a trigger and activated the Nephilim gene at the young adult age of twenty years old.

"And Cush the son of Ham, the son of Noah, took a wife in those days in his old age, and she bare a son, and they called his name Nimrod, saying, At that time the sons of men again began to rebel and transgress against God, and the child grew up, and his father loved him exceedingly, for he was the son of his old age.

And the garments of skin, which God made for Adam and his wife, when they went out of the garden, were given to Cush. For after the death of Adam and his wife, the garments were given to Enoch, the son of Jared, and when Enoch was taken up to God, he gave them to Methuselah, his son.

And at the death of Methuselah, Noah took them and brought them to the ark, and they were with him until he went out of the ark. And in their going out, Ham stole those garments from Noah, his father, and he took them and hid them and hid them from his brothers. And when Ham begat his firstborn Cush, he gave him the garments in secret, and they were with Cush many days. And Cush also concealed them from his sons and brothers, and when Cush had begotten Nimrod, he gave him those garments through his love for him, and Nimrod grew up, and when he was twenty years old he put on those garments. And Nimrod became strong when he put on the garments, and God gave him might and strength, and he was a mighty hunter in the earth, yea, he was a mighty hunter in the field, and he hunted the animals and he built altars, and he offered upon them animals before the Lord" (Jasher 7:23-30).

In *The Jewish Encyclopedia*, Nimrod's description reads "His great success in hunting was to the fact that he wore the coat of skin which God made for Adam and Eve" (Genesis 3:21). Jewish scholars believe that the garments of skin possessed special powers. Moses, the author of the book of Genesis, says, "The Lord God made for Adam and his wife garments of glory, for the skin of their flesh, and He clothed them" (Genesis 3:21 ESV).

The words "skin" and "light" are the same in the pre-Canaanite context. According to the Zohar, "We are not to imagine that prior to the 'garments of skin' made by God for Adam and Eve that they were utterly naked.

On the contrary, their original garb, like that of Aaron in the Tabernacle, consisted of light, in consonance with the purity of their earthly paradise. In Hebrew the words for light and skin are homonyms, both pronounced or but spelled differently, light with the alef and skin with an ayin. That linguistic kinship enabled the Zohar to soar: by sinning, Adam and Eve had their garments of celestial light replaced by 'garments of skin,' which merely protected but no longer illuminated. Indeed, it was not their exterior which had mutated. Beyond paradise, there was neither comfort nor security nor wisdom" (Zohar. ll, 229a-b).

Through scripture, it is evident that when Adam and Eve walked in the Garden, they were created in the image of God. They were given celestial garments, which illuminated the glory of God from within, and when they sinned, they mutated from within, for the glory of God had departed. However, God still had a plan of redemption and made them garments of skin, light, or glory for protection.

"So God created man in His own image, in the image of God He created him; male and female He created them" (Genesis 1:17 NIV).

20 Scriptures in the Bible tell us that God is light. "This is the message we have heard from Him and announce to you, that God is light, and in Him, there is no darkness at all" (1 John 1:5 KJV).

When Adam and Eve sinned, the light/glory departed; because of their genetic mutation, darkness now existed, and they were no longer in the image of God. God put them out of the Garden because of their disobedience, but not without His garments of glory.

"And Nimrod became strong when he put on the 'garments of glory,' and God gave him might and strength" (Jasher 7:30). He began to become a giant after he put on the garments of Adam, "suggesting a similar role to Jabal, Jubal, and Tubal-Cain, 'fathers' of all herders, musicians, and metalworkers," the first at their professions, and Nimrod the "first mighty hunter."

In the book of Daniel, King Nebuchadnezzar becomes a beast: "Let his heart be changed from man's, and let a beast's heart be given unto him; and let seven times pass over him. This matter is by the decree of the watcher, and the demand by the word of the holy ones: to the intent that the living may know that the most High ruleth in the kingdom of men. And giveth it to whomsoever he will, and setteth up over it the beast of men" (Daniel 4:16-17 KJV).

The book of Daniel is clear that the judgment of King Nebuchadnezzar was by proclamation of the Watcher angels. He was part beast and part human. He was charged to live as a human hybrid for seven years because of his disobedience. After seven years, his humanity was restored.

The Bible reveals that humans can live as a human hybrid because of sin or genetics/DNA, so was Nimrod a giant/hybrid? I believe Nimrod inherited genetics/DNA and experienced trauma that caused a trigger, which activated the Nephilim gene in him at the young adult age of twenty years old. He began to become a giant after he put on the garments of Adam or the 'garments of glory.'

The life of Nimrod starts to take a very diabolical turn as the inherited genetics/DNA is triggered. He is now a human hybrid, establishes idolatry, becomes the first prosecutor of God in this Nephilim gene, conquers cities, and becomes the mighty hunter, now of human souls. He is the fifth ruler of the first Postdiluvian area of Uruk/Iran.

"And they found a large valley opposite to the east, and they built him a large and extensive city, and Nimrod called the name of the city that he built Shinar, for the Lord had vehemently shaken his enemies and destroyed them. And Nimrod dwelt in Shinar, 'Freemason's' and he reigned securely, and he fought with his enemies and he subdued them, and he prospered in all his battles, and his kingdom became very great. And all the nations and tongues heard of his fame, and they gathered themselves to him, and they bowed down to the earth, and they brought him offerings, and he became their Lord and king, and they all dwelt with him in the city at Shinar, and Nimrod reigned in the earth over all the sons of Noah, and they were all under his power and counsel.

And all the earth was of one tongue and words of union, but Nimrod did not go in the ways of the Lord, and he was more wicked than all the men that were before him, from the days of the flood until those days. And he made gods of wood and stone, and he bowed down to them, and he rebelled against the Lord, and taught all his subjects and the people of the earth his wicked ways; and Mardon his son was more wicked than his father" (Jasher 7:43-47).

"This principle took its ground in Nimrod, that great monarch and first establisher of idolatry, and the first grand persecutor of God in his select seed, 'Antichrist' or a hunter of souls; therefore called the mighty hunter before the Lord... This Nimrod, having the fullness of the angels' nature in him, made him exceedingly proud, thinking himself equal with God." [5]

"And the whole earth was of one language, and of one speech. And it came to pass, as they journeyed from the east, that they found a plain in the land of Shinar; and they dwelt there. And they said one to another, Go to, let us make brick, and burn them thoroughly. And they had brick for stone, and slime had they for mortar. And they said, 'Go to, let us build us a city, a tower, whose top may reach unto heaven; and let us make a name, lest we be scattered abroad upon the face of the whole earth'" (Genesis 11:1-4 KJV).

Shinar and the Freemasons are connected historically with empires that were in rebellion against God, from its association with Babylon's wickedness and the worship of other gods in the last days and the end times. "And he called out with a mighty voice, "Fallen, fallen is Babylon the great! She has become a dwelling place for demons, a haunt for every unclean spirit, a haunt for every unclean bird, a haunt for every unclean and detestable beast. For all nations have drunk the wine" (Revelation 18:2-3 ESV).

Shinar is also the location of Judah's exile when they are taken into Babylonia, where King Nebuchadnezzar took precious items from the Lord's temple and placed them in the house of the god that he worshiped.

"In the third year of the reign of Jehoiakim king Judah, Nebuchadnezzar king of Babylon come to Jerusalem and besieged it. And the Lord gave Jehiakim king of Judah into his hand, with some of the vessels of the house of God. And he brought them to the land of Shinar to the house of his god, and placed the vessels in the treasury of his god" (Daniel 1:1-2 NIV).

In the last days, Shinar (Freemasons) has its association with the Antichrist and has always been connected to the world's rebellion against God and the formation of a one world government. It is the location of the Tower of Babel, and even with the wickedness in Shinar, God will have a faithful remnant of Israel, the "Root of Jesse," and all the nations will gather unto Him, speaking of the Messiah.

"In that day the root of Jesse, who shall stand as a signal for the peoples— of him shall the nations inquire, and his resting place shall be glorious"

(Isaiah 11:10). In the last days, God will demonstrate His redemptive power to the Jewish nation, and as they gather in Shinar to worship Jesus in His millennial kingdom, God will show His redemptive grace for His church, the Bride.

Through Biblical history, we know that the structure of the Tower of Babel was erected in the land of Shinar or Babylonia in a time period after the deluge. We know that Nimrod and the Babylonians wanted to build a city and a tower/temple, a gateway, or a portal to reach the heavens, which is the first principle of Freemasonry. Babylonia occupied the southeastern Mesopotamian region between the Tigris and Euphrates Rivers, known to us today as southern Iraq around Baghdad to the Persian Gulf.

"And the whole earth was of one language, and of one speech. And it came to pass, as they journeyed from the east, that they found a plain in the land of Shinar; and they dwelt there. And they said one to another, Go to let us make brick, and burn them thoroughly. And they had brick for stone, and slime had they for mortar. And the Lord came to see the city and the tower, which the children of men builded" (Genesis 11:1-5 KJV).

As we continue to study Biblical history, we know that Nimrod did not stop with his conquest of Babylon. Still, he was famous for his conquest of Assyria and the construction of Nineveh. The great Assyrian was a hunter for souls, but he will always be remembered and famous for constructing the Tower of Babel, a gateway or portal reaching into the heavens, because of the strong principalities and demonic presence.

The Tower of Babel is the type of altar or system that the Antichrist will erect in the last days, a one world government and a one world religion. Nimrod is a type of the Antichrist, or "the Beast," and through Freemasonry, there have been monuments and places of worship erected throughout the world that inhabit these demonic principalities that are rooted in this secret society in which they want to rule and govern the world.

The principle behind the Tower of Babel and the structure of Freemasonry is to connect our world to the principalities of the second heaven through these portals or gateways. "And they worshiped the dragon, who had given authority to the beast; and they worshiped the beast, saying, 'Who is like unto the beast? Who is able to make war against it?'" (Revelation 13:4 BSB).

One of the first things the Bible is very informative about is the material used to construct the Tower of Babel. The primary materials used were brick. The Hebrews, while under Egyptian bondage, had learned the process of brick making, and since Shinar was in Babylon, we know because history tells us that the process of making bricks was very ancient.

"The Septuagint specifies, 'Their mortar was Bitumen,' translated as 'tar' above. Bitumen is a black, oily, gelatinous, and highly flammable material. It is also known as tar or asphalt and had many uses in the ancient world. It is known to have been in use by Neanderthals as an adhesive to fix handles onto their tools. Some scholars claim Bitumen has been in use for some 40,000 years and is closely related to petroleum, oil, and sulfur." [6]

The Babylonians used Bitumen to build buildings, roadways, houses, boats, and walls to hold the floodwater from the Euphrates River.

"The Greek historian Herodotus (484 to 425 BC) writes about deposits of asphalt in the city of Hit in Mesopotamia: 'There is a city eight days journey from Babylon, where a little river named 'Is' flows, a tributary of the Euphrates River. From the source of this little river gouts (drops or spots) of asphalt rise with the water, and from thence the asphalt is brought for the walls of Babylon.'" [7]

The use of Bitumen was very common in this region and is one of the logical reasons why Nimrod would have chosen to build the Tower of Babel here. Why would Nimrod want to build a waterproof tower? Through historical research, we now know that it was meant to be a temple/altar or portal/gateway. Through historical and Biblical research, the building or the temple/altar was in remembrance of the 200 Watchers and the Nephilim who perished during the deluge.

"And they said on to another, Go to, let us build us a city and a tower, whose top may reach unto heaven; and let us make us a name, lest we be scattered abroad upon the face of the whole earth" (Genesis 11:4 KJV).

When we look at the paradigm of Nimrod and the Tower of Babel, he did not only want to reach the heavens by building the temple/tower. He was also adamant in trying to obtain mortality by creating a gateway or an illegal portal by honoring and offering sacrifices to the "200 Watchers that left their first estate," and perished in the deluge. "The principalities of the air," and the Nephilim, and did not want to be "scattered abroad upon the face of the whole earth."

An interesting fact about these "200 Watchers that left their first estate" and "the principalities of the air": the Nephilim did not want to be "scattered abroad upon the face of the whole earth." In the United Nations, there are 193 countries that the United Nations recognizes, and then there are places like Taiwan, Palestine, Vatican City, U.N., Puerto Rico, Guam, American Samoa, Northern Ireland, the Canary Islands, Tibet, Nepal, Greenland, and Iceland, an independent European nation, and about 13 countries that are not recognized but are connected to other countries. For example, Puerto Rico is a territory of the United States; Taiwan and Nepal are considered to be a part of the People's Republic of China; Palestine is recognized because of Israel, the Vatican City resides in Europe, Northern Ireland, along with Scotland, Wales, and even England are all part of the United Kingdom, and Greenland is part of the Kingdom of Denmark, be consistent with scripture in the book of Genesis.

"And they said one to another, Go to, let us build us a city and a tower, whose top may reach unto heaven; and let us make us a name, lest we be scattered abroad upon the face of the whole earth" (Genesis 11:4). Could it be possible that the principalities of the Tower of Babel, the spirits of the 200 Watchers, are scattered among the nations of the earth to control certain regions and territories in "heavenly places?" "When the Most High gave to the nations their inheritance, when he divided mankind, he fixed the borders of the people according to the number of the sons of God" (Deuteronomy 32:8 ESV).

"And he made gods of wood and stone, and he bowed down to them, and he rebelled against the Lord, and taught all his subjects and the people of the earth his wicked ways; and Mardon his son was more wicked than his father" (Jasher 7:47). Nimrod made gods of wood and stone, and he worshiped them depicting his outright rebellion against God.

Nimrod and this Postdiluvian population were in rebellion towards God and did not adhere to His authority but established a government and a religion that opposed the mind and heart of God. 200 angels, principalities, and rulers of darkness gathered in this region to oppose the "Supreme Elohim." The Bible tells us that Nimrod wanted to build a tower/temple "whose top may reach unto the heavens."

This tower would dominate this region socially and spiritually. It would symbolize Nimrod, an "Antichrist," leading a revolt against God and going against God's command concerning subduing and replenishing the earth. Because of his rebellion by uniting these people against God, he was going to deal with the judgment of God, like the generation in Genesis 1:2 and the generation of Noah.

"Many Jewish scholars in their writings have accepted this truth; Nimrod wanted to avenge the fallen angels and the Nephilim." The ancient historian Josephus states of Nimrod, "He also said he would be revenged on God, if He should have the mind to drown the world again; for that he would build a tower too high for the waters to be able to reach and that he would avenge himself on God for destroying their forefathers." [8]

The fourth Angelic Invasion, are the angels bound in the Euphrates river. While many believe the identity of these four angels remain unclear, the mystery of these angels is intriguing as they are bound to the Euphrates river. The Bible gives us a glimpse of who they are. In the book of Daniel, in chapter 10, it mentions that the Prince of Persia withstood Daniel's prayers for three weeks. The Apostle Paul in the book of Ephesian 6:12 states this prince was a principality spirit, the highest ranking angel in the demonic kingdom who resided and controlled Babylon (Iraq) and when Baylon fell this Prince had to be bound or imprisoned. The Bible mentions four empires, The Babylonian Empire (Iraq), The Persian Empire (Iran), The Roman Empire (Europe, North Africa, and Middle East) and the Grecian Empire (Greece, Southern italy, Asthenia Minor, Ionia, Aeolia, Doris, and all the colonies around the Mediterranean) all had a ruling principality, high ranking angels that when these empires were conquered they had to be imprisoned or bound somewhere in the earth which I believe there is Biblical evidence is the Euphrates River.

In the book of Daniel, it states that Daniel dreamed of four beasts, "Daniel said: 'In my vision at night I looked, and there before me were the four winds of heaven churning up the great sea. Four great beasts, each different from the others, came up out of the sea.

The first was like a lion, and it had the wings of an eagle. I watched until its wings were torn off and it was lifted from the ground so that it stood on two feet like a human being, and the mind of a human was given to it.

And there before me was a second beast, which looked like a bear. It was raised up on one of its sides, and it had three ribs in its mouth between its teeth. It was told, 'Get up and eat your fill of flesh!'

After that, I looked, and there before me was another beast, one that linked like a leopard. And on its back it had four wings like those of a bird. This beast had four heads, and it was given authority to rule.

After that, in my vision at night I looked, and there before me was a fourth beast-terrifying and frightening and very powerful. It had large iron teeth, it crushed and devoured its victims and trampled underfoot whatever was left. It was different from all the former beasts, and it had ten horn's" (Daniel 7:2-7).

"I approached one of those standing there and asked him the meaning of all of this. So he told me and gave me the interpretation of these things: The four great beasts are four kings that will rise from the earth"(Daniel 7:16-17).

The four beasts represent four kings that will rise from the earth, the lion represents Babylon (Iraq), the bear represents Persia (Iran), the leopard represents Greece, the dragon represents Rome, and the ten horns represent divided Europe. (Shocking Discovery: Who Are The Fallen Angels In The Euphrates River? Written and Produced by Glorious Mandate, February 2023).

In the book of Revelation, the Apostle John gives us a narrative of the four beasts that come out of the sea at the time of the tribulation when the Antichrist comes into power. As the coalitions of these countries gather together to form a One World Government, these four high ranking demonic angels will be unleashed from the Euphrates river to kill a third of the human race (Revelation 9:15).

The interesting thing about this angelic rebellion is that when it occurs, it happens to be located where Nimrod led a rebellion against God with the Tower of Babel which is located on the Euphrates river (2 Kings 24:7). We now have biblical evidence why these four high ranking angels decided to defect from their place in heaven, and reside and control these regions and demonic kingdoms.

These fallen angels end time assignment and purpose is to kill a third of the human race (Hebrews 2:14). Why they are bound in the Euphrates "into to chains of darkness, to be reserved unto judgment" (2 Peter 2:4 KJB), is unclear but is it possible that they may have assisted Nimrod with the technology on how to build a stargate/portal to gain access into the heavenly realm as they are connected to Babylon (Genesis 11:9).

"And the Lord came down to see the city and the tower, which the children of men builded, And the Lord said, Behold, the people is one, and they have all one language; and this they begin to do: and now nothing will be restrained from them, which the children of men builded" (Genesis 11: 5-6). The Biblical description of the Tower of Babel through Moses's writings lets us know that this tower was unlike anything man had built on earth or anything God had ever seen on the face of the earth. He came down from heaven to observe what Nimrod had built.

"And the Lord said, 'Behold, the people is one, and they have all one language; and this they begin to do: and now nothing will be restrained from them, which they have imagined doing. Go to, let us go down, and there confound their language, that they may not understand one another's speech'" (Genesis 11:5-7 ESV).

And it came to pass that because of Nimrod's rebellion, and to prevent further idolatry and moral degradation of this society, God chose to confuse their language. "When the Most High (Supreme Elohim) gave the nations their inheritance, when he divided all mankind, he set up boundaries for the peoples (dispersed the people) according to the number of the sons of Israel (sons of God/200 Watchers that rebelled)" (Deuteronomy 32:8 ASV).

The original translation of Deuteronomy 32:8 read sons of God, not the sons of Israel; a slight error was lost in the translation.

In understanding the proper narrative and chronological events of the Bible and the context of this scripture, Israel did not exist when the Tower of Babel occurred. We have to refer to the genealogy of the Bible: the Tower of Babel event took place before year 2008 BC, which is about the time that Abraham was born.

Going back from there, we trace Abraham's genealogy to Peleg, who was born in the year 1757 BC, about 10 years after the flood. In Genesis 11, the Bible emphasizes the genealogy of Abram's family as Terah becomes the father of Abram, the birth of Israel occurs years after the Tower of Babel.

The narrative of Genesis 10:8-12 is incorrect in its translation because of the chronological period of Israel. "When the Most High (Supreme Elohim) gave the nations their inheritance, when he divided all mankind (Tower of Babel), he set up boundaries for the people (dispersed the people) according to the number of the sons of Israel (or the sons of God/the 200 Watchers that rebelled)" (Deuteronomy 32:8 NRSV).

This scripture should read, "He set up boundaries for the people according to the number of the sons of God" (Deuteronomy 32:8; the Masoretic Text translation). "Rabbinic Judaism—traditionally adheres to the first interpretation, with some exceptions, and modern Jewish translations may translate Bnei Elohim as 'sons of rules' rather than 'sons of God.' Regardless, the second interpretation (sons of angels or other divine beings) is nonexistent in modern Judaism. This is reflected by the rejection of Enoch and other Apocrypha supporting the interpretation from the Hebrew Bible Canon. In some versions of Deuteronomy, the Dead Sea Scrolls refer to the sons of God rather than the sons of Israel, probably in reference to angels. The Septuagint reads similarly." [9]

Because of doctrine and religion, even though the Masoretic Text and the Septuagint translations may be different, it may have been done intentionally because of the rejection of angels taking human women as wives, the Book of Enoch, and other Apocrypha supporting Genesis 6:2.

The principalities and powers of the air that formed a powerful nation as Nimrod erected the Tower of Babel and were dispersed in the boundaries that were set up, and they became nations throughout the earth. Israel is birthed after the Tower of Babel at the birth of Abraham.

Gilgamesh/Nimrod's tomb was found in Iraq, and the Giant Skelton was retrieved in 2003 to find the Nephilim's DNA genome.[10] Archaeologists strongly believe that this is the lost tomb of Nimrod, who built the Tower of Babel for possible future DNA engineering. Hormuzd Rassm found a book called *The Epic of Gilgamesh*, which shows evidence that King Nimrod/

Gilgamesh lived in Uruk/Iraq and was buried by the Euphrates River, where his body was found.

Some clay tablets were found in the book *The Epic of Gilgamesh*. These tablets confirm what Biblical scholars and historians believe, that Nimrod was buried under the Euphrates in Uruk/Iraq, and scientists believe these are the remains of Nimrod the Nephilim. Scientists believe that the possibility of finding "this ancient city under the Iraqi desert" was only made possible through the advancement of modern technology.[11]

Gilgamesh and Nimrod have been compared to each other, and historians and scholars believe they were two thirds god/Anunnaki and one third human/Homo sapiens. They were hybrids, part angelic and part human. This belief comes from polytheism, which is the belief that multiple deities assembled into a pantheon of gods to create a religion or a sect.

In light of Nimrod and the Nephilim DNA, scientists have begun the research of "genetic manipulation and epigenetic research" to acquire DNA for the possible resurrection and retrieval of the Nephilim DNA genomes. Could this be Babylon rising in the last days, "the return of the Nephilim"?

Could it be that the corporation that is taking the lead on this research is pushing for the fulfillment of the end time prophecy by modifying human DNA through a vaccine called the "biometric vaccine"? Could this be the return of human hybrids, and once again, creation is being threatened by the Nephilim DNA genomes through genetic manipulation and the creation of a new species on the face of the earth? (Possibly the mark of the Beast.)

We know that "When human beings began to increase in number in the earth and daughters were born to them, the sons of God saw that the daughters of humans were beautiful, and they married any of them they chose" (Genesis 6:1-2). As the "sons of God" married the daughters of Adam, they had children, and the by-product of this abomination altered the DNA of God's creation. These children (a new species) were called the Nephilim, "the mighty men who were of old, the men of renown."

"The universal sentiment of the Masons of the present day is to confer upon Solomon, King of Israel, the honor of being their 'First Grand Master.' But the LeGenesisd of the Craft had long before, though there was a tradition of the temple extant, bestowed, at least by implication, that title upon Nimrod, 'The Master Architect,' the King of Babylonia and Assyria. It attributed the first organization of a fraternity of craftsmen to him, saying that he gave a charge to the workmen whom he sent to assist the king of Nineveh in building his cities" (i) (Genesis x. 8-12) (ii) The late George Smith, of the British Museum, the author of "Assyrian Discoveries," of the "Chaldean Account of Genesis," and many other writings in which he has the result of his investigations of the cuneiform inscriptions.[12]

"Just as it was in the days of Noah, so also will it be in the days of the Son of Man" (Luke 17:26).

13

WALLS OF JERICHO

According to the biblical account, when Joshua and Caleb entered the Levant after Jericho, they circled the walls seven times, causing them to crumble. While some may interpret this as an act of genocide, the narrative suggests a different motive; the eradication of the Nephilim seed, the Gibborim giants.

The city of Jericho was once known as the "City of Giants." The Gibborim Giants inhabited it in Joshua's time. 5,000 years before Uruk, Jericho was the first settlement city surrounded by walls. It is one of the oldest cities, from about 10,000 BC to the present.

The Bible tells us in the book of Joshua that Joshua, the military Commander, and Moses's aide, recalls the events surrounding the walls of Jericho: "Now Jericho was straitly shut up because of the children of Israel: none went out, and none came in" (Joshua 6:1 KJV).

And the Lord said unto Joshua, See, I have given into thine hand Jericho, and the king thereof, and the mighty men of valour. And ye shall compass the city, all ye men of war, and go round about the city once. Thus shalt thou do six days? And seven priests shall bear before the Ark seven trumpets of rams' horns: and the seventh day ye shall compass the city seven times, and the priests shall blow with the trumpets. And it shall come to pass, that when they make a long blast with the ram's horn, and when ye hear the sound of the trumpet, all the people shall shout with a great shout; and the wall of the city shall fall down flat, and the people shall ascend up every man straight before him. And Joshua the son of Nun called the priests, and said unto them, Take up the Ark of the Covenant, and let seven priests bear seven trumpets of rams' horns before the Ark of the Lord. And he said unto the people, Pass on, and compasses the city, and let him that is armed pass on before the Ark of the Lord. And it came to pass, when Joshua had spoken unto the people, that the seven priests bearing the seven trumpets of rams' horns passed on before the Lord, and blew with the trumpets: and the Ark of the Covenant of the Lord followed them.

And the armed men went before the priests that blew with the trumpets, and the reward came after the ark, the priests going on, and blowing with the trumpets. And Joshua had commanded the people, saying, Ye shall not shout, nor make any noise with your voice, neither shall any word proceed out of your mouth, until the day I bid you shout; then shall ye shout. So the Ark of the Lord compassed the city, going about it once: and they came into the camp, and lodged in the camp. And Joshua rose early in the morning, and the priests took up the Ark of the Lord. And priests bearing seven trumpets of rams' horns before the Ark of the Lord went on continually, and blew with the trumpets: and the armed men went before them; but the reward came after the Ark of the Lord, the priests going on, and blowing with the trumpets. And the second day they compassed the city once, and returned into the camp: so they did six days. And it came to pass on the seventh day, that they rose early about the dawning of the day, and compassed the city after the same manner seven times: only on that day they compassed the city seven times. And it came to pass at the seventh time, when the priests blew with the trumpets, Joshua said unto the people, Shout; for the Lord hath given you the city. And the city shall be accursed, even it, and all that are therein, to the Lord: only Rahab the harlot shall live, she and all that are with her in the house, because she hid the messengers that we sent. And ye, in any wise keep yourselves from the accursed thing, lest ye make yourselves accursed, when ye take of the accursed thing, and make the camp of Israel a curse, and trouble it. But all the silver, and gold, and vessels of brass and iron, are consecrated unto the Lord: they shall come into the treasury of the

Lord. So the people shouted when the priests blew with the trumpets: and it came to pass, when the people heard the sound of the trumpet, and the people shouted with a great shout, that the wall fell down flat, so that the people went up into the city, every man straight before him, and they took the city. And they utterly destroyed all that was in the city, man and woman, young and old, and ox, and sheep, and ass, with the edge of the sword. But Joshua had said unto the two men that had spied out the country, Go into the harlot's house, and bring out thence the woman, and all that she hath, as ye swore unto her. And the young men that were spies went in, and brought out Rahab, and her father, and her mother, and her brethren, and all that she had; and they brought out all her kindred, and left them without the camp of Israel. And they burnt the city with fire, and all that was therein: only the silver, and the gold, and the vessels of brass and of iron, they put into the treasury of the house of the Lord.

And Joshua saved Rahab the harlot alive, and her father's household, and all that she had; and she dwelleth in Israel even unto this day; because she hid the messengers, which Joshua sent to spy out Jericho. And Joshua adjured them at that time, saying, Cursed be the man before the Lord, that riseth up and buildeth this city Jericho: he shall lay the foundation thereof in his firstborn, and in his youngest son shall he set up the gates of it. So the Lord was with Joshua; and his fame was noised throughout all the country (Joshua 6:1-27 NKJV).

The Bible clarifies that God was angry and commanded Joshua to destroy Jericho. According to the 1901 Jewish Encyclopedia, the king of Jericho, Shobach, was as famous for his strength as Goliath and the Ammonites. The "Gibborim Giants" were the offspring of the Nephilim giants mentioned in Genesis 6 but were not as powerful or tall. However, history and the Bible tell us they were still dangerous and mighty warriors.

The Nephilim in the book of Genesis were the offspring of the Watcher's "fallen angels" as they procreated and started to change the DNA makeup of God's creation by taking human women and creating a new species, the "Gibborim." According to theologians and Biblical scholars, Gibborim is the same Hebrew word used by Moses in Genesis 6:4 about "the mighty men," the giants.

"And the Lord said unto Joshua, See, I have given into thine hand Jericho, and the king thereof, and the mighty men of valour" (Joshua 6:2).

The Bible tells us that the "Gibborim Giants" inhabited the city of Jericho. When the walls of Jericho fell, the "Gibborim" confronted Joshua and Israel in a great battle.

"There were giants in the earth in those days; and also after that, when the sons of God came in unto the daughters of men, and they bare children to them, and the same became mighty men which were of old, men of renown" (Genesis 6:4 KJV).

Megalithic structures/cyclopean technology include the Wall of Jericho and the Pyramids. These structures are believed to be pre-deluge, meaning they were erected sometime before the Great Flood. The Nephilim and their offspring built these structures.

The technologies of the fallen angels built these megalithic structures to align with the stars, astrology, and astronomy.

"A megalithic stone is a large stone that has been used to construct a prehistoric structure or a monument either alone or together with other stones. There are over 35,000 in Europe alone, located widely from Sweden to the Mediterranean Sea." [1]

Before the flood, the earth had what we call the Greenhouse Effect, which created an atmosphere that enabled animals and plants to grow enormously because of the warm tropical environment, which enhanced oxygen levels. "And God said let there be a firmament, in the midst of the waters, and let it divide the waters from the waters. And God made the firmament, and divided the waters which were under the firmament from the water which were above the firmament: and it was so" (Genesis 1:6-7 KJV).

This atmosphere created a vapor canopy created by God. "And God made the firmament and divided the waters from the water" (Genesis 1:7 KJV).

In the book of Genesis, God informs Noah of His plan to bring about a flood, a devastating event that would eliminate all flesh with the breath of life. In response, Noah, a man of faith, begins to build an ark. On the seventeenth day of the second month, the ark is completed, and Noah and his family enter it. "On that very day, all the springs of the great deep burst forth, and the floodgates of the heavens were opened. And the rain fell on the earth forty days and forty nights" (Genesis 7:11-12 NIV).

"Citing evidence of denser atmosphere in the past, Morris postulated that this vapor layer could have dramatically increased the atmospheric pressure on the surface of the early earth, again contributing to a healthier environment (like a natural hyperbaric chamber)." [2]

As we embark on our journey through the Bible's historical events, we are captivated by the intricate interweaving of the Bible and archeology. With each revelation, we are brought closer to the hidden truths that illuminate our past, our present, and the future that awaits God's creation. It's a truly awe-inspiring experience, witnessing the prophecies of the Bible unfold in real time through the lens of archeological discoveries.

Consider the profound significance of the structure and remains of the walls of Jericho. Archeologists, driven by a shared curiosity, have meticulously sliced trenches deep into this mound, revealing 23 successive settlements built atop each other. The oldest layer, a testament to the depth of history we are exploring, dates back to 8000 BCE. A large retaining wall at the base of the embankment, constructed from Cyclopean stone, stands as a tangible link to biblical narratives and prophecies, underscoring the weight of these historical findings.

The Cyclopean wall also supported a second mud brick wall at the height of 8 meters. Was the great wall of Jericho built in the time of Ahab and Jezebel, or did the Nephilim build them in a time before the great deluge? The Lexham Bible Dictionary states, "The final Bronze Age City of Jericho wall, referred to as a Cyclopean Wall, encapsulates the city, and its construction dates to Middle Bronze III around 1600 BC. Cyclopean masonry is a type of stonework found in Mycenaean architecture, built with massive limestone boulders, roughly fitted together with minimal clearance between adjacent stones and with clay or mortar." [3]

True Cyclopean architecture is not from the Middle Bronze Age, but actual Cyclopean structures date back before the Great Flood, which means they were part of the foundation of the walls of Jericho built by the Nephilim before the flood.

"In the 1950s, Kenyon, a British archaeologist, was teaching Levantine archaeology at University College, London, when John Garstang a British archaeologist, an excavator of Jericho, who had searched for the tumble down walls of Jericho, asked her to review the pottery he had found in Jericho. Her conclusion; his evidence for the walls of Jericho were not compelling. As newly appointed director of the British School of Archaeology in Jerusalem, Kathleen Mary Kenyon initiated a new excavation project in Jericho in 1952 and found that Garstang's dates for the destruction of the site's fortifications had been grossly wrong." [4]

One of the most compelling discoveries by archaeologist Kenyon suggests that the earliest wall of the wall of Jericho dates to around 8000 BC, and she based this on radiocarbon technology.

"Radiocarbon dating is a method that provides objective age estimates for carbon-based materials that originated from living organisms. An age could be estimated by measuring the amount of carbon-14 present in the sample and comparing this against an internationally used reference standard." [5] There is some controversy with carbon dating, but it does date the Cyclopean architecture used on the walls of Jericho to be pre-deluge.

The ancient city of Jericho, once home to a race of giants, boasts polygonal stonewalls that defy the ages. These walls, believed to be the work of the extinct Nephilim/Cyclops, continue to intrigue scholars, historians, philosophers, and archaeologists.

While many modern scholars have overlooked the Megalithic structures scattered across the globe, a new generation, driven by a thirst for divine truths, is beginning to uncover their significance. These structures, including the walls of Jericho, hold the key to understanding the eternal struggle between good and evil since the fall of Lucifer.

Jericho, with its Cyclopean architecture, stands as a testament to a bygone era. Its foundation, shrouded in mystery and believed to have a demonic origin, is a marvel of ancient engineering. This city, with one of the oldest protective walls in the world, continues to fascinate historians and archaeologists alike.

The city of Jericho was impossible to penetrate, for it had become a "City of Giants," and the Gibborim Giants inhabited it in the days of Joshua.

The Book of Joshua recounts how Joshua, Moses's military commander and personal aide, reflects on the events surrounding the walls of Jericho. This city, chosen by God for conquest, was a city of giants and demonic principalities, a city that had been a stronghold since the time of the Nephilim. It was a city that Joshua, invoking a curse, ensured would not be rebuilt since the time of the great flood, a testament to the historical significance of Jericho.

"And Joshua charged them at that time, saying, 'Cursed be the man before the Lord, who riseth up and buildeth this city Jericho: he shall lay its foundation with his firstborn, and with his youngest he shall set up the gates'" (Joshua 6:26). Excavations revealed the city of Jericho had been built many times before the story of Joshua when the Israelites marched around the city seven times, rendering its destruction.

"The largest of these settlements was constructed in 2600 BCE by the Amorites. About 2300 BCE, there was once more a break in the site's occupation. It was taken over by the Canaanites in 1900 BCE and reached its greatest prominence between 1700 BCE NS 1550 BCE."[6]

The Canaanites were known for idolatry, and they worshiped the idol named Molech, the god of fire. Molech was a Canaanite deity associated with the practice of child sacrifice and linked to the Old Testament worship of the popular god Baal.

Molech was a foreign god given an illegitimate place of worship in Israel, and God was particular when He gave the laws to Moses, forbidding the Jews to participate in any worship in Egypt or Canaan.

"Do not permit any of your children to be offered as a sacrifice to Molech, for you must not disgrace the name of your God. I am the Lord" (Leviticus 18:21 NLT). This generation of mothers who worshiped Moloch would roll their babies into the fire as a sacrifice.

Archaeologists have discovered excavations and revealed the remains of babies burned and later embedded in the walls of Jericho, which is evidence of the demonic stronghold in this city from when the Nephilim inhabited the City of Giants.

There is Biblical evidence that this was a Canaanite practice: sacrificing children to idols in ancient Israel. The Bible speaks of passing children to Molech, and the prophetic literature speaks about the "passing of sons and daughters through the fire" (2 Kings 16:3, 17:7, 21:6, 23:10; Numbers 31:23).

Many other Biblical texts confirm this Nephilim practice associated with Baal, which speaks of the sacrifice of children, even to Yahweh; Psalms 106:37-38, Jeremiah 7:31, Ezekiel 20:25-26, 16:21, 20:32, 23:37, and 39 all speak of sacrificing children. This Canaanite practice of worshiping these unnamed idols can be traced back to the Watchers and the Nephilim.

"And all the others together with them took unto themselves wives, and each chose for himself one, and they began to go in unto them and to defile themselves with them, and they taught them charms and enchantments, and cutting of roots, and made them acquainted with plants. And they became pregnant, and they bare great giants, whose height was three thousand ells: Who consumed all the acquisitions of men. And men could no longer sustain them, the giants turned against them and devoured mankind. And they began to sin against birds, and beasts, and reptiles, and fish, and to devour one another's flesh and drink the blood. Then the earth laid accusation against the lawless ones" (Enoch 7:1-6 Translated by RH Charles, D. Litt., DD).

The book of Hosea states, "My people are destroyed for lack of knowledge: because thou hast rejected knowledge, I will also reject thee, that thou shalt be no priest to me: seeing thou has forgotten the law of thy God, I will also forget thy children" (Hosea 4:6 KJV).

Witchcraft, deeply rooted in the history of the Watchers, demands our immediate attention. Our ignorance of scripture and historical and archaeological events has allowed the practices of Baal, Molech, and the Nephilim to infiltrate our culture and society. This has, in turn, unleashed a demonic presence, wreaking havoc on our children and future generations. The scripture calls us to action, "For we wrestle not against flesh and blood but against principalities, against powers, against the rulers of the darkness of this world, against spiritual wickedness in high places" (Ephesians 6:12 NIV).

Archaeologists unearthed a Neolithic settlement in Jericho, a clear manifestation of a demonic stronghold and a military fortress. This was not just a city, but an altar of defiance against the God of Israel. The city of Jericho, preparing for war, was warned: "Listen, O Israel! Today, you are about to cross the Jordan River to take over the land belonging to nations much greater and more powerful than you. They live in cities with walls reaching the sky" (Deuteronomy 9:1 NLT).

Archaeologists have found and confirmed that the "city walls of Jericho reached the sky" and "the mound, or 'tell,' of Jericho was surrounded by a great earthen rampart, or embankment, with a stone retaining wall at its base. The retaining wall was some 12-15 ft high; on top was a mudbrick wall 6 ft thick and about 20-26 ft high."[7]

The Gibborim Giants, the offspring of the Watchers and the Nephilim, inhabited the City of Giants. Joshua knew there were supernatural powers at work in the region not visible in the earthly realm that was waging war against God's people, and he put out a decree: "Cursed be the man before the Lord who rises up and builds this city Jericho; he shall lay its foundation with his firstborn, and with his youngest he shall set up its gates" (Joshua 6:26 KJV).

Joshua warned that if anyone attempted to rebuild this city, their oldest son would die at the time of the reconstruction of Jericho, and if he persisted in erecting this citadel, he would also attend the funeral of his youngest.

In the book of 1 Kings, Jeremiah writes about Hiel the Bethelite: "In his days did Hiel the Bethelite build Jericho: he laid the foundation thereof in Abiram his firstborn, and set up the gates thereof in his youngest son Segub, according to the word of the Lord, which he spoke by Joshua son of Nun" (1 Kings 16:34 KJV). Joshua decreed the city of Jericho never to be rebuilt and warned what would happen to anyone who tried. As a result, Hiel the Behelite does not heed his warning and decides to rebuild the city. He laid the foundations, and his first son, Abram, perished, and when the gates were erected, he lost his youngest son, Segub.

The city of Jericho had been built and destroyed many times before the story of Joshua, when the Israelites marched around the city seven times, causing its destruction. But here's a thought-provoking question: How were the Nephilim, the giants of old, able to move these massive stones and place them in their exact positions? This intriguing aspect of the story invites us to delve deeper into the mysteries of the biblical narrative

The cyclopean architecture used the walls of Jericho to be pre-deluge; these stones were cut from massive, solid rocks without using any mortar and were fitted together.

Many theologians, historians, and archaeologists believe the technology possessed by the giants who built these megalithic structures was the knowledge given to them by the Watchers, as recorded in the Book of Enoch. These were fallen angels who possessed superior strength, intelligence, and technology.

Archaeologists have found that there is coloration with many of the megalithic structures worldwide. Their technology cannot be duplicated by modern science and is more advanced than modern technology and science.

Scientists have discovered resonating energy from these structures while conducting harmonic and electromagnetic experiments. I believe the Nephilim who built these structures used cymatics and harmonics to levitate and cut these stones with such precision.

"Steve Quayle states in his investigation that the Incas, Aztecs, and Mayans, especially the giants that would move stones which are found in Latin America and South America, have some of the most amazing pieces of architecture, and it was stated that the Nephilim nasopharyngeal passage could create sound that would offset the gravity or a gravity field that would move these stones." [8]

Cymatics "is the study of visible sound vibration and shows the transformational nature of sound and matter. Sound guides us and shapes, yet it is an intangible force." [9]

"A harmonic is a wave or signal whose frequency is an integral (whole number) multiple of the frequency of the same reference signal or wave as part of the harmonic series or wave. As part of the harmonic series, the term can also refer to the ratio of the frequency of such a signal or wave to the frequency of the reference signal or wave." [10]

Is it possible that the Nephilim were using Nephilim cymatics and harmonics produced by their Nasopharyngeal passage to create a sound that would offset the gravity or a gravity field that would move and cut stones? From the beginning of time, sound has always been instrumental; as we look at the book of Genesis, we know that God spoke the world into existence (Genesis 1:3-29 KJV).

The Creator of the universe demonstrated divine cymatics and harmonics as He created the world by speaking it into existence. The Nephilim learned this technology from the Watchers, who learned it from God, their Creator, as they observed Him speak the world into existence with sound waves and vibration.

God, in all His wisdom, was about to demonstrate to the "Gibborim Giants," who inhabited Jericho, "The City of Giants," that it would be destroyed with the same technology they had learned from the Watchers. The Lord instructed Joshua, "See, I have given into thine hand Jericho, and the king thereof, and the mighty men of valor. And ye shall compass the city, all ye men of war, and go round about the city once. Thus shalt thou do six days? And seven priests shall bear before the Ark seven trumpets of rams' horns: and the seventh day ye shall compass the city seven times, and the priests shall blow with the trumpets. And it shall come to pass, that when they make a long blast with the ram's horn, and when ye hear the sound of the trumpet, all the people shall shout with a great shout; and the wall of the city shall fall down flat, and the people shall ascend up every man straight before him" (Joshua 6:3-5 KJV).

Later in the chapter, we read about how, on the seventh day, Joshua and his men were able to destroy the walls of Jericho and conquer the city using the same technology that the Nephilim used to build this demonic city. The destruction of the city prevented future generations from mingling with Nephilim DNA. It kept Rahab's DNA from being contaminated, as she

THE ORIGIN OF SIN

became part of the lineage of Jesus Christ, "the Messiah" (Matthew 1:5-6 KJV).

"And it came to pass on the seventh day, that they rose early about the dawning of the day, and compassed the city after the same manner seven times: only on that day they compassed the city seven times. And it came to pass at the seventh time, when the priests blew with the trumpets, Joshua said unto the people, Shout; for the Lord hath given you the city" (Joshua 6:15-16 KJV). God gave them a sound because heaven moves by sound since the beginning of time.

This city had such a demonic Nephilim stronghold that Joshua was instructed not to take any of the spoils of war as the people of God were accustomed to whenever they conquered a city.

"And the city shall be accursed, even it, and all that are therein, to the Lord: only Rahab the harlot shall live, she and all that are with her in the house, because she hid the messengers that we sent. And ye, in any wise keep yourselves from the accursed thing, lest ye make yourselves accursed, when ye take of the accursed thing, and make the camp of Israel a curse, and trouble it. But all the silver, and gold, and vessels of brass and iron, are consecrated unto the Lord: they shall come into the treasury of the Lord" (Joshua 6:17-19 KJV).

This city was such an offense to God, which He confirmed when He stated "The city shall be accursed to the Lord." This meant that he didn't want the people to touch or take anything from the city because it was a Nephilim demonic citadel. God didn't want His people to take anything that carried a demonic stronghold into their lands or homes.

"For we wrestle not against flesh and blood" (Ephesians 6:12).

14

GOLIATH THE NEPHILIM

The tale of Goliath, the Nephilim giant, has endured for over 3,000 years. While some may dismiss it as a mere children's fable, akin to "Jack and the Beanstalk," it is, in fact, a living testament to the perpetual conflict between the forces of good and evil that has spanned the ages.

Embark on a journey through the life of Goliath, the most renowned giant in history, and discover the truth of the relentless war between the giants and the children of God. The Israelites have long associated them with the Nephilim giants of Genesis, from the antediluvian age (Genesis 6:1).

"Goliath was a son of the Giant in Garth, the 'son of Rapha,' of the Anakim and the descendants of Anak, and his three sons, Sheshai, Ahiman, and Talmai. They ascended by the south, and came unto Hebron; now Hebron was built seven years before Zoan in Egypt" (Numbers 13:22 KJV).

"And there we saw the giants, the sons of Anak, which come of the giants: and we were in our sight as grasshoppers, and so we were in their sight" (Numbers 13:33 KJV). Goliath, the most renowned of all giants, is a figure you've likely encountered in the Bible story of David and Goliath. As we've explored in previous chapters, giants have been a constant presence in our narrative, vehemently opposing God's creation and His people.

"Goliath the Gittite," therefore Goliath, was a son of "the giant in Gath" who had four brothers, Lahmi, Saph-Sippal, Ishbibenob, and the name of the fourth brother is unknown.

In Joshua 14, the Anakites appear but not in the same locations; Once again, there was a battle between the Philistines and Israel. David went down with his men to fight against the Philistines and became exhausted. And Ishbi-Benob, one of the descendants of Rapha, whose bronze spearhead weighed three hundred shekels [b] and who was armed with a new sword, said he would kill David. But Abishai, son of Zeruiah came to David's rescue; he struck the Philistine down and killed him. Then David's men swore to him, saying, "Never again will you go out with us to battle, so that the lamp of Israel will not be extinguished." In the course of time, there was another battle with the Philistines, at Gob. At that time Sebeka the Hushathite killed Saph, one of the descendants of Rapha. In another battle with the Philistines at Gob, Elhanan son of Jair [c] the Bethlehemite killed the brother of [d] Goliath the Gittite, who had a spear with a shaft like a weaver's rod. In still another battle, which took place at Gath, there was a huge man with six fingers on each hand and six toes on each foot—twenty-four in all. He also was descended from Rapha. When he taunted Israel, Jonathan, son of Shimeah, David's brother, killed him. These four were descendants of Rapha in Gath, and they fell at the hands of David and his men (2 Samuel 21:15-22 KJV).

The Israelites' unsuccessful conquest against the Anakites had profound implications. The Anakites, having repelled the Israelites, established their presence in Gath and the surrounding areas, which would later evolve into the land of the Philistines, a significant turning point in biblical history.

Joshua, in his account, claimed to have eradicated all of the Anakites and triumphed over the "Northern Kingdoms" to secure the Promised Land "as the Lord commanded Moses" (Joshua 11:20). However, his narrative of conquest was marred by his failure to fully obey the Lord. He allowed the Anakites to inhabit the lands of Garza, Gath, and Ashdod, and even permitted them to live in close proximity to the Philistines, the sworn enemies of the Israelites, a decision that would have significant repercussions.

"At that time Joshua went and destroyed the Anakites from the hill country: from Hebron, Debir and Anab, from all the hill country of Judah, and from all the hill country of Israel. Joshua totally destroyed them and their towns. No Anakites were left in Israelite territory; only in Gaza, Gath, and Ashdod did any survive" (Joshua 11:21-22 NIV)

According to Caleb, they have now appeared on the country's hillside in a greatly fortified city. Caleb recalls his promise to God and defeats the Anakites, as he recalls the 40 years of wandering in the wilderness. Before entering the wilderness, God had commanded them to spy out the land that flowed with milk and honey. Still, because of their negative report, they did not possess the land but were struck by a plague and died. Only Joshua and Caleb of all the men that went to spy on the land remained alive (Numbers 14:36-38).

"The Amalekites dwell in the land of the south: and the Hittites, and the Jebusites, and the Amorites, dwell in the mountains: and the Canaanites dwell by the sea, and by the coast of Jordan. And Caleb stilled the people before Moses, and said, Let us go up at once, and possess it; for we are well able to overcome it. But the men that went up with him said, We are not able to go up against the people; for they are stronger than we. And they brought up an evil report of the land which they had searched unto the children of Israel, saying, The land, through which we have gone to search it, is a land that eateth up the inhabitants thereof; and all the people that we saw in it are men of a great stature. And there we saw the giants, the sons of Anak, which come of the giants: and we were in our own sight as grasshoppers, and so we were in their sight" (Numbers 13:29-33 KJV).

"In accordance with the Lord's command to him, Joshua gave to Caleb son of Jephunneh a portion in Judah—Kiriath Arba, that is, Hebron. (Arba was the forefather of Anak.) From Hebron Caleb drove out the three Anakites—Sheshai, Ahiman and Talmai, the sons of Anak" (Joshua 15:13-14 NIV).

Goliath and his brothers lived during a time of significant turbulence; the descendants of Anak occupied the Promised Land. In Numbers 13:22, 28, and 33, they are described as giants, and as Canaanites, they were descendants of Ham. Goliath was a Philistine, a people group that Genesis 10:13 says were descended from Ham's offspring in Egypt

"Egypt was the father of the Ludites, Anamites, Lehabites, Naphtuhites, Pathrusites, Kasluhites (from whom the Philistines came) and Caphtorites. Canaan was the father of Sidon his firstborn, and of the Hittites, Jebusites, Amorites, Girgashites, Hivites, Arkites, Sinites, Arvadites, Zemarites and Hamathites. Later the Canaanite clans scattered, and the borders of Canaan reached from Sidon toward Gerar as far as Gaza, and then toward Sodom, Gomorrah, Admah and Zeboyim, as far as Lasha. These are the sons of Ham by their clans and languages, in their territories and nations" (Genesis 10:13-20 NIV).

At its core, this narrative revolves around the giants and the Israelites, with Moses playing a pivotal role. It was he who instructed them to spy on the holy land, selecting one man from every tribe for this task. These men spent 40 days scouting out "the land that flowed with milk and honey." The subsequent 40 years of wandering in the wilderness led to a momentous clash between good and evil, mirroring the 40 days the spies spent in a land filled with despair, fear, and darkness.

Following 40 days of reconnaissance in the Promised Land, the spies returned with contrasting reports. The majority delivered a negative report, stating they could not capture the land due to the giants in their fortified cities. Fear seized the people of God, and they began to lament, "If only we had died in the land of Egypt!" In stark contrast, Joshua and Caleb gave a positive report, affirming, "The land we passed to scout is a good land that flows with milk and honey; God will bring us to this land and give it to us" (Numbers 13-14 CSB).

God spared the children of Israel but did not allow them to enter the Promised Land because of their unbelief when they encountered the Nephilim giants. They would wander in the desert for the spies' unbelief every day.

Goliath was in a locked conflict with the Israelites. He was an intimidating force and an imposing figure to all who came in contact with him. This giant descendant of the Nephilim was about nine feet tall and mocked the Israelites and their armies daily.

"A champion named Goliath, who was from Gath, came out of the Philistine camp. His height was six cubits and a span. He had a bronze helmet on his head and wore a coat of scale armor of bronze weighing five thousand shekels [b]; on his legs he wore bronze greaves, and a bronze javelin was slung on his back. His spear shaft was like a weaver's rod, and its iron point weighed six hundred shekels. [c] His shield bearer went ahead of him" (1 Samuel 17:4-7 NIV).

Goliath wore armor from his head down to his feet; this giant was very versed in the art of war, and he was a champion, meaning that this was not his first time in battle. When we look at the word "champion," it means "a person who has defeated and surpassed all in a competition." [1]

This was not Goliath's first battle; I'm sure this was not the first time he "mocked the Israelites and their armies." He approached them wearing his garments of war, an oversized coat with overlapping bronze rings. This coat shielded him from his shoulders down to his knees and was designed to protect him from any weapons of war.

The Bible tells us that his copper coat of scale armor weighed "5,000 shekels," which now equates to about 200 pounds. This did not include the helmet he was wearing, the bronze greaves he wore on his legs, and the bronze javelin strapped to his back. The head of the spear alone weighed about 600 shekels, which would equate to about 25 pounds. His spear shaft was like a weaver's rod, and its iron point weighed 600 shekels.[c] His shield bearer went ahead of him (1 Samuel 17:4-7 NIV).

Could you imagine the sight of Goliath as he stood before the Israelites and taunted David? How could the people of God send a young shepherd boy to confront the Philistine champion in front of all those assembled on the battlefield? Goliath had a reputation; he was a champion, not just a Philistine champion, but also a Nephilim Champion.

To have a better understanding of the giant Goliath, we know that he and his brothers were the descendants of Anak, who occupied the Promised Land of Canaan, and that they were the descendants of Ham. The book of Genesis tells us that Ham is "the second son of Noah and the father of Cush, Mizraim, Phut, and Canaan." [2]

The existence of Goliath and his brothers can also be traced back to the Moabites. In the book of Ruth, the Bible tells readers the narrative of two Moabite women, Ruth and Orpah, and their mother-in-law, Naomi.

"In the days when the judges ruled, [a] there was a famine in the land. So a man from Bethlehem in Judah, together with his wife and two sons, went to live for a while in the country of Moab. The man's name was Elimelek, his wife's name was Naomi, and the names of his two sons were Mahlon and Kilion. They were Ephrathites from Bethlehem, Judah. And they went to Moab and lived there. Now Elimelek, Naomi's husband, died, and she was left with her two sons. They married Moabite women, one named Orpah and the other Ruth. After they had lived there about ten years, both Mahlon and Kilion also died, and Naomi was left without her two sons and her husband" (Ruth 1:1-5 NIV).

Naomi is now confronted with the reality that she is left with two Moabite women to care for. She receives the news in Moab which is modern day Jordan that the Lord has provided food and decides that she will return to her homeland, Judah (Ruth 1:6-7).

As this narrative unfolds, we know that Naomi confronts her daughters-in-law and advises them to "Go back to their mother's home in hope that they would find another husband. Naomi kissed both of them as she wept, and they said they would go back with Naomi and her people" (Ruth 1:8-10 NIV).

Orpah, the sister of Ruth, is the second character in the narrative of the book of Ruth; she is the second daughter-in-law of Naomi. Unlike Ruth, who decides to stay with her mother-in-law, "She kissed Naomi goodbye and went back to her people and her gods" (Ruth 1:14-15 NIV).

The Moabites were a by-product of an incestuous relationship between two daughters. They perpetuated their family lineage by conceiving sons after a diabolical plot to get their father drunk. The oldest daughter named her son Moab, and he became the father of a powerful nation, the Moabites, who came from the loins of Lot after he fled from Sodom and Gomorrah with his two daughters.

Lot, who had obtained wealth and "had flocks and herds and tents," found himself in a difficult situation. It was not in his best interest to continue to move about with Abram, his uncle, because the number of flocks and herds they owned was placing a strain on the land, and he could no longer support them staying together. The Bible tells us that Lot pitched his tents near Sodom, a decision that would later prove to be a grave one as "the people of Sodom were wicked" (Genesis 13:13), their wickedness reaching a level that could no longer be ignored.

What was going on in Sodom and Gomorrah that got the Host of Heaven's attention, so much so that God wanted to destroy the city? Is there a correlation here with the Nephilim of Genesis 6:5?

"The Lord saw how great the wickedness of the human race had become on the earth. And that every inclination of the thoughts of the human heart was only evil. The Lord regretted that he had made human beings on earth, and his heart was troubled. So the Lord said, 'I will wipe from the face of the earth the human race I have created—and with them the animals, the birds and the creatures that move along the ground—for I regret that I have made them'" (Genesis 6:5-7 NIV).

The Lord was so angry about the behavior of Sodom and Gomorrah that he sent angels to destroy this perverse and wicked city like he destroyed the earth with the flood because of the unnatural behavior and genetic alteration influenced by the Nephilim.

"And the angels who did not keep their proper domain, but left their own abode, He has reserved in everlasting chains under darkness of the judgment of the great day; as Sodom and Gomorrah, and the cities around them in a similar manner to these, giving themselves over to sexual immorality and gone after strange flesh, are set as an example, suffering the vengeance of eternal fire" (Jude 1:6-7 NKJV).

Orpah's narrative is based on her promiscuous actions, and her descendants depict her in an unfavorable light. Once she had taken leave of her mother-in-law, her subsequent actions were deemed extremely negative. She is said to have lain that night with one hundred men and even with a dog. The Philistine Goliath, who fought the young David during the battle of Elah, was born of this promiscuous activity. (Ruth Rabbah 2:20).

Orpah's wanton behavior is said to be characteristic of her, and one of the exegeses of her name describes such conduct: "Orpah—because everyone ground her like bruised corn [harifot]." [3]

Orpah gives herself over to sexual immorality and strange flesh and gives birth to Nephilim giants. She is the mother of the Philistine giant, Goliath, and his four brothers. Ruth is the mother of Obed, and Jesse is the son of Obed and the father of King David, who is the great-grandson of Boaz and Ruth. Orpah and Ruth were sisters-in-law because they were both married to Naomi's sons.

But in Rabbinic literature, "The Rabbis maintain that Orpah and Ruth were sisters, the daughters of King Eglon of Moab" (Ruth Rabbah 2:9). [4]

According to The Shalvi/Hayman Encyclopedia of Jewish Women, King David and Goliath, the Champion Philistine/Nephilim, were cousins.

The Babylonian Talmud (Sotah 42b) makes Goliath a descendent of Orpah and also makes Orpah and Ruth sisters (in the Bible, they are only sisters-in-law). Goliath, the Nephilim giant, and David, future king of Israel—a battle that represented the reality of the war between the forces of good and evil.

15

THE RETURN OF THE NEPHILIM

"An Angelic Invasion"

"But as the days of Noah were, so shall the coming of the Son of man be" (Matthew 24:37 KJV).

To investigate and summarize God's unfolding theme in the Bible storyline, we must first examine the narratives of "the seed of the woman" and "the seed of the serpent" in light of the Old and New Testaments.

"And I will put enmity between you and the woman, and between your seed and her seed; He shall bruise you on the head, and you shall bruise him on the heel." (Genesis 3:15 NASB). God makes an underlying declaration in Genesis 3: a prophetic declaration that He will be in opposition with Satan and his seed for generations until the culmination of the final judgment, Armageddon.

Prophetically, the Godhead lets Satan and "the principalities, the powers, the rulers of darkness, and the spiritual wickedness in high places" know that there will be a death blow to the powers of darkness. This was very disturbing to Satan; now he's aware of a "man-child" that will be born and bruise his head.

In this prophetic declaration, we also know that Satan will deliver a blow to the seed of the woman and "bruise him on the heel." In the natural, it would seem like a death blow. In this blow, when Jesus is on the cross, "one of the soldiers pierced His side with a spear," and a miracle occurs: "And out of His side, blood and water gushed out."

The only time scientifically when water and blood are gushing out of a person is when a woman gives birth to a child. This is a significant event that we can recognize and know it's time for the child to be delivered. In a similar way, when Christ, referred to as "the seed of the woman," was crucified, blood and water gushed out. This was a symbolic birth of the church. The blood represented the redemption of His creation, as He had dealt with the sins of the fall of man. As it's written, "The law requires that nearly everything be cleansed with blood, and without the shedding of blood there is no forgiveness" (Hebrews 9:22 NIV).

As we step into an era of technological advancement, transhumanism, UFOs, aliens, and alien encounters, the body of Christ must not only keep an open mind but also recognize its role. The water imparted life to the church; through death, life produced the most powerful entity God created, the church, which is not only relevant but also a powerful force in these times.

"To make her holy, cleansing her by washing with the water through the word" (Ephesians 5:26 NIV).

Humanity races towards the last days; we have been given a powerful tool through "the seed of the woman," the church, as we enter the age of the return of the Nephilim. The Nephilim, often interpreted as fallen angels or giants, are a significant part of biblical history and their return signifies a crucial period in the end times.

The current events unfolding across the globe are not mere coincidences. They bear a profound significance, one that your worldview may hinder your perception of. However, it's of utmost importance that we delve into what the Bible has to say about these present times and the future events that the world and the church will face. As it's written, "He that answereth a matter before he heareth it is folly and shame unto him" (Proverbs 18:13 KJV). This is a call to open our minds and hearts to the wisdom of the Scriptures.

In the days of Noah, about 200 angels, also known as Watchers, looked down into the Earth. They saw "the daughters of men," and decided that they would cohabitate with these women. This decision led to the creation of a new hybrid species, which was an attempt to alter the DNA of God's creation. This event, known as the Nephilim incident, is a significant part of biblical history and has implications for our understanding of the end times.

We know that Shemihazah and Asael, the leaders of the second invasion of 200 Watchers, which caused iniquity on the Earth during the time of Noah, have been placed in prison under the Earth. This prison, known as Dudael, is a place of darkness with sharp rock. They will remain there until the appointed time of judgment, which is a significant event in the end times (Enoch 10:4-7).

"These are the generations of Noah; Noah was a just man and perfect in his generations, and Noah walked with God" (Genesis 6:9 KJV). The word perfect in this verse is tamiym, which means Noah and his family were genetically pure without blemish; his genealogy was untainted.

Today, scientists are experimenting with the human genome and attempting to produce human hybrids, both biological and mechanical, by splicing genes together. "The Human Genome Project (HGP) is an international collaboration that successfully determined, stored, and rendered publicly available the sequences of almost all the genetic content of the chromosomes of the human organism, otherwise known as human genome."[1]

Scientific technology is advancing at an alarming rate as scientists race towards producing a new species of human "hybrids" that will be more advanced physically, intellectually, biologically, and mechanically. We will see the birth and marriage of nanotechnology, genetics, robotics, artificial intelligence, and neuralink technology that will produce a new superhuman being as we enter the last days before the coming of the Messiah.

Ray Kurzweil states, "If we apply these principles at the highest level of evolution on Earth, the first step, the creation of cells, introduced the paradigm of biology. The subsequent emergence of DNA provided a digital method then, the evolution of a species that combined rational thought with an opposable appendage (i.e., the thumb) caused a fundamental paradigm shift from biology to technology. The primary paradigm shift will be from biological thinking to a hybrid combining biological and no biological thinking. This hybrid will include 'biological inspired' processes resulting from reverse engineering of biological brains." [2]

There is a great deception coming as we approach these last days. Many will be deceived, just as Satan deceived the ancient world through genetic manipulation by corrupting that world with the Nephilim seed and enticing them with technology. As we enter an era of technological advancement, transhumanism, UFOs, aliens, and alien encounters, these will be used to deceive the very elect, once again, by corrupting humanity's DNA. "For there shall arise false Christ and false prophets, and shall shew great signs and wonders, insomuch that, if it were possible, they shall deceive the very elect" (Matthew 24:24 KJV).

The conflict between two seeds has been at war since the beginning. The first prophecy we were given was concerning "the seed of the serpent" and "the seed of the woman." As we look at the language, it speaks prophetically about God's redemptive plan (Genesis 3:15).

With technological advancement in recent years, many have turned to social media, like Facebook, Instagram, Twitter, and TikTok. Especially in recent years, with the COVID-19 pandemic, many are leaving the local church for spiritual guidance and using this technological growth to stay away from the local church.

They are creating a platform for themselves by moving in signs and wonders, prophecy, word of knowledge, and the gift of healing. We have witnessed many false Christs, false prophets, and false teachers. But what spirit is ministering behind these false prophets and false teachers? A spirit of divination and witchcraft has entered the church. Pastors and ministers are prostituting their gifts and have perverted the altar, even deceiving those in the "body of Christ." Technology has amplified an existing problem within the church: the wheat and the tares growing together. In this time of crisis, we must remember our unity, our shared responsibility to protect and uphold the true teachings of Christ.

Another parable He put forth to them, saying. "The kingdom of heaven is like a man who sowed good seed in his field; but while man slept, his enemy came and sowed tares among the wheat and went his way. But when the grain had sprouted and produced a crop, then the tares also appeared. So the servants of the owner came and said to him, 'Sir, did you not sow good seed in your field? How then does it have tares?' He said to them, 'An enemy has done this.' The servants said to him, 'Do you want us then to go and gather them up?' But he said, 'No, lest while you gather up the tares you also uproot the wheat with them. Let both grow together until the harvest, and at the time of harvest I will say to the reapers, 'First gather together the tares and bind them in bundles to burn them, but gather the wheat into my barn'" (Matthew 13:24-30 NKJV).

The World Economic Forum and Scientific American convene once a year and make predictions about how scientific advancements and emerging technologies will affect the world we live in socially and economically.

They have intensely focused on artificial intelligence, genetic engineering, self-healing material, systems metabolic engineering, body adapted wearable electronics, personalized medicine, and genomic vaccines. While I believe that technology has assisted and will assist humanity with a better quality of life, the result will be used to corrupt God's creation and create a new hybrid species, bringing about the return of the Nephilim.

UFOs, aliens, and alien encounters: the Bible never gives us any indication that angels descend upon the earth with wings. When we look at the idea of aliens, the proper description would be that an alien is an extraterrestrial, or interdimensional not of the earth but from different dimensions or other worlds. They are sentient beings.

What I mean by sentient being is "the capacity to have feelings, experience sensations and emotions." [3] You and I are sentient beings from another dimension that have teleported to this Earth through the portal process; of human birth by the conception of a man and a woman becoming one. We are the human scientific fingerprint of God, His creation.

"For you created my inmost being; you knit me together in my mother's womb. I praise you because I am fearfully and wonderfully made; your works are wonderful, I know that full well" (Psalms 139:13-14 NIV). In the book of Psalms, David lets us look into the genetic disposition of the characteristic of the human DNA, as God formed him in his mother's womb.

"Therefore a man shall leave his father and his mother and hold fast to his wife, and they shall become one flesh" (Genesis 2:24). Our spirit teleported into our mother's womb, where God formed our flesh: "Before I formed you in the womb I knew you, before you were born I set you apart; I appointed you as a prophet to the nations" (Jeremiah 1:5 NIV).

Similarly, we will be changed and teleported to the heavens when God comes for us: "Listen, I tell you a mystery; We will not all sleep, but we will all be changed, In a flash, in the twinkling of an eye, at the last trumpet. For the trumpet will sound, the dead will be raised imperishable, and we will be changed. For the perishable must cloth itself with the imperishable, and the mortal with immortality" (1 Corinthians 15:51-53 NIV).

The Bible is adamant in this narrative in informing the children of God that we are not of this world. There are 20 Scriptures in the Bible, in the Old and New Testament, that verify that you and I are not from this world but from a different dimension: Romans 12:2, 12:1-2, 1:20, 14:1-23; John 18:36; 1 John 2:5, 2:15-17, 5:19, 2:17, 4:5, 3:13, 2:16, 4:4, 5:4, 2:15-16, 4:1, 3:1, 2:2, 5:6, 1:7; John 17:14, 17:18, 8:23, 15:18-19, 3:16, 17:15, 15:18-21, 8:12, 14:27, 16:33, 16:11, 18:37, 12:46, 14:30, 12:31, 17:14-16, 13:18, 7:7, 1:11; Colossians 3:2, 2:8; James 4:4, 1:27; Ephesians 6:12, 5:11; Philippians 3:20-21, 3:20; Revelation 21:1-27; Matthew 6:24, 7:16-20,16:26, 13:22, 11:11; 1 Peter 2:11, 5:8; 2 Corinthians 10:3, 5:20; Titus 2:11; 2 Peter 1:4; Proverbs 23:17; 1 Corinthians 3:19, 3:18, 1:28-29, 15:33, 1:13; Luke 1:37, 1:35; Hebrews 13:5; Mark 8:36, 16:15; 1 Timothy 6:7; 1 Peter 4:3; Psalm 31:19; Ephesians 2:19-21; Jeremiah 29:11; Isaiah 45:1; Daniel 7:13; 2 Peter 3:9; Revelation 1:1-20; 1 Peter 2:9; Hebrews 13:14; Ephesians 2:2; John 17:18; Luke 19:10; Titus 2:12; 1 Timothy 6:10; John 17:17, 16:3; Matthew 1:18; Genesis 25:18; Mathew 21:22, 17:11-23; Exodus 20:25; 2 Corinthians 5:17; John 4:1-54.

"If you were of the world, the world would love you as its own; but because you are not of this world, but I chose you out of the world, therefore the world hates you" (John 15:19 ESV). The Bible clearly informs humanity that other sentient beings exist, like the "four creatures" and "the twenty-four elders."

"Surrounding the throne were twenty-four other thrones, and seated on them were twenty-four elders. They were dressed in white and had crowns of gold on their heads. From the throne came flashes of lightning, rumblings, and peals of thunder. In front of the throne, seven lamps were blazing. These are the seven spirits of God. Also, in front of the throne was what looked like a sea of glass, clear as crystal.

In the center, around the throne, were four living creatures, and they were covered with eyes, in front, and in back. The first living creature was like a lion, the second was like an ox, the third had a face like a man, and the fourth was like a flying eagle. Each of the four living creatures had six wings and was covered with eyes all around, even under its wings. Day and night, they never stop saying: 'Holy, holy, holy is the Lord God Almighty, who was, and is, and is to come'" (Revelation 4:4-8 NIV).

When the Watchers descended to Mount Harmon (through a portal), some believe they could have arrived in spaceships, "chariots of fire." Biblical scholars may debate this view. Still, as we studied the evidence and the language of scripture, it is possible that the Watchers could have arrived in some flying craft through teleportation on Mount Harmon. Mt. Hermon comes from the semitic root word HERM which means taboo, also called Baal-Herman or Baals Taboo Mountain in Judges 3, this place is known as one of the most evil places on the earth. "In 1869 on the summit of Mt. Hermon, in Israel, British explorer Sir Charles Warren came across a temple, and found a limestone stele which may be the only extra- biblical and pagan memorial of Satan's actual command to the Sons of God to create a hybrid race, that is inscribed with an oath that the watchers made with each other to corrupt the genetics "DNA" of the human race and to teach them forbidden knowledge." [4]

The Bible gives us an example of teleportation when Philip is transported miraculously after the Ethiopian was baptized: "And when they were come up out of the water, the Spirit of the Lord caught away Philip, that eunuch saw him no more; and he went on his way rejoicing. But Philip was found at Azotus: and passing through he preached in all the cities, till he came to Caesarea" (Acts 8:39-49 KJV).

There are many examples of portals in the Bible; Jacob's ladder is a perfect example of a portal: "And he dreamed, and behold a ladder set up on the earth, and the top of it reached to Heaven, and the angels of God were ascending and descending on it" (Genesis 28:12 ESV).

The Bible tells us that sentient beings have been teleporting from the beginning of time; this is alien/angel technology. Scientists today have become obsessed with human innovation and alien technology; they pursue technological advancement like "CERN." But this is not about "CERN," but a portal to alternate dimensions, creating wormholes for teleportation.

The Lord visits Jacob in a dream, and this dream has prophetic implications with the idea that there are portals or gateways used by the angels of God as a means of travel when they enter and leave the realm of the Earth. "And Jesus answered him, Blessed are you, Simon Bar-Jonah! For flesh and blood has not revealed this to you, but my Father who is in heaven, And I tell you, you are Peter, and on this rock, I will build my Church, and the gates of hell shall not prevail against it. I will give you the keys of the kingdom of heaven, and whatever you bind on Earth shall be bound in heaven and whatever you loose on Earth shall be loosed in heaven" (Mathew 16:17-19 ESV).

The landscape and the narrative of Matthew 16 concerns the kingdom and the gates of hell, or portals. The Bible tells us that hell is within the earth, the lower "parts" of the earth. There are many realms within the belly of the earth.

Both gates and hell are used in the plural, meaning that there are many portals or gateways to the belly of hell; hell is within the Earth, as the Bible describes. Abraham's bosom is a part of hell that was reserved for those pre-Christ Christians: "And it came to pass, that the beggar died, and was carried by the angels into Abraham's bosom: the rich man also died, and was buried" (Luke 16:22 KJV).

The reality is that there are many portals to hell. It is Biblical that there are different locations in hell that house its prisoners according to their crimes: "And, behold, the veil of the temple was rent in twain from the top to the bottom; and the earth did quake, and the rocks rent; And the graves were opened, and many bodies of the saints which arose, And came out of the graves after His resurrection, and went into the holy city, and appeared unto many" (Matthew 27:51-53 KJV).

There is a kingdom in heaven where the King of heaven sits on the throne, and in the hierarchy of the heavens, "When the veil tore from top to bottom the graves opened. And the saints who rose from the dead were teleported into the holy city"(Matthew 27:51-53). And portals opened at the first resurrection and came out after Christ's resurrection.

The apostle John writes to the seven churches in Asia Minor, in the book of Revelation 3:1-6, that stands out but not for anything good. The outer appearance of the church seemed like a healthy church but was dead inside. When we look at the letters to the seven churches Sardis and Laodicea receive condemnation, the spiritual condition of the church in Sardis was a gateway to hell.

No one can enter a city without the jurisdiction of these elders. These seats were thrones. In the book of Revelation 3, the city of Sardis, an ancient city in what is now Turkey, was home to the well-known temple of Arthemis; in the Greek religion, she was a goddess. With the worship of these pagans' gods, there was a gateway or an open portal into the city to the gates of hell. Much like the city of Sardis, CERN is a portal gateway; The Large Hadron Collider was fired up for the third time as scientists searched for "new physics.

Run by the European Organization for Nuclear Research, or CERN, the Large Hadron Collider near Geneva, Switzerland, is at the forefront of global scientific exploration. Its purpose is to allow scientists to test theories and predictions of particle physics and find new physics, shaping our understanding of the universe.[5]

After a long hiatus to improve the upgrade data collection and detectors, the Large Hadron Collider is at it again. The journal *Nature* reports that the first two operational runs tested and explored "known physics."The discovery of the Higgs Boson particle, or "god particle," in 2012 was part of that work and reaffirmed current models of how the universe works. This time, they are looking for new physics and unknowns, such as dark matter.

But some people are worried about what is going on at CERN. Social media has been exploding with theories, often with a version of the claim, "They are hiding this from you." "One of the most popular theories is that CERN is using the Large Hadron Collider to open portals to another plane, a parallel universe, or some stargate. Or CERN is trying to create black holes. This stems from CERN saying it might be possible to create tiny black holes but tried to clear that statement up." [6]

"On 10 September 2002, Switzerland became a full member of the United Nations, the United Nations Office at Geneva, Switzerland, in one of the four major offices of the United Nations." [7]

The Bible tells us what CERN is attempting to achieve and that it has already existed from the beginning of time: there are portals or gateways to hell and portals to heaven where the Holy City is.

The understanding that there are worlds and different dimensions is a Biblical reality from the beginning of time. The Bible is clear that "the gates of hell, portal, or gateways shall not prevail against His church,"(Matthew 16:18 KJV). The existence of portals to these realms may be a new concept to the scientist from CERN. Who is experimenting with opening portals to hell and other dimensions? "I know where you dwell, where Satan's throne is. Yet you hold fast my name, and you did not deny my faith even in the days of Antipas my faithful witness, who was killed among you, where Satan dwells" (Revelation 2:13 NSAV).

The Apostle John gives us some incredible insight concerning the location of "Satan's throne and where Satan dwells." To better understand this revelation, we must look into who Antipas is and what occurred when and where he was killed. It is believed, according to Eastern Orthodoxy, that during the reign of Nero, he was put to death at the "Appollyon temple" in a brazen, bull-shaped altar. As we look into the location of where CERN is located in the town called "Saint-Genesisus-Polly" in Geneva, Switzerland, the name "Polly" derives from the Latin word *ppolliacum*, and it is, I believe, where the temple of Apollo existed during the time of the Romans.

The Apostle John gives us some insight concerning the end times and the bottomless pit and the angel who has the keys to open the bottomless pit.

"And the fifth angel sounded, and I saw a star fall from heaven unto the earth: and to him was given the key of the bottomless pit. And he opened the bottomless pit; and there arose a smoke out of the pit, as the smoke of a great furnace; and the sun and the air were darkened by reason of the smoke of the pit, And they had a king over them, which is the angel of the bottomless pit, whose name in the Hebrew tongue is Abaddon, but in the Greek tongue his name is Apollyon" (Revelation 9:1-2, 11 KJ21).

As we continue to advance in technology, is CERN opening portals for time travel, or is it a gateway for "the angel of the bottomless pit whose name in the Greek is Apollyon"?

We are living in an incredible time period concerning the end time events prophesied throughout the 66 books of the Bible. The Bible makes it clear in the book of Matthew: "And I say also unto thee, That thou art Peter, and upon this rock I will build my church; and the gates of hell shall not prevail against it" (Matthew 16:18 KJV).

The Book of Enoch states when the Watchers/fallen angels arrived on Earth, they took wives, making a covenant with these women and their fathers, and they bargained with humanity and revealed to men the forbidden secrets that they were striving to learn. Have modern day scientists and the secret society that exists made a covenant with Satan and created a portal (CERN) to hell or Tartarus in an attempt to free the angels that left their habitation and created horrific crimes against humanity?

These secrets revealed to humanity are what we would today call science, technology, and human innovation. The sons of Adam authorized this union by willfully giving their daughters to the sons of God, "the Ancient Race," in exchange for technology.

"Lamech married two women, one named Adah and the other Zillah. Adah gave birth to Jabal; he was the Father of those who live in tents and raise livestock (Real Estate & Farming), His brother's name was Jubal; he was the Father of all who play stringed instruments and pipes. Zillah also had a son, Tubal-Cain, who forged all kinds of tools out of bronze and iron. Tubal-Cain's sister was Naamah" (Genesis 4:19-22 NIV).

Human innovation results from the Watchers teaching humans innovation through science and technology. The descendants of Cain became the forefathers of innovation, as they mastered the arts of real estate, farming, music, instruments, tools, and weapons. By mastering the elements of the earth, since man was cursed through agriculture, they willfully gave themselves over to technology.

"To Adam, God said, 'Because you listened to your wife and ate fruit from the tree about which I commanded you, 'You must not eat from it; 'Cursed is the ground because of you; through painful toil you will eat food from it all the days of you life'" (Genesis 3:17 NIV).

UFOs, aliens, and alien encounters have been occurring at such a high degree of consistency and have been witnessed by civilians worldwide. But what truly underscores the importance of these events is the confirmation by the U.S. Military and the persistence of individuals like Harry Reid. "The Department of Defense confirmed what seekers of extraterrestrial life have long hoped to be accurate; they're real. Navy pilots spoke about objects that seemed to defy the laws of physics. Details emerged about a mysterious, five-year Pentagon program and claims that metal alloys have recovered from unidentified phenomena. The former Senate Majority Leader Harry Reid, a staunch advocate, spoke about his long push for more research on unidentified flying objects." [8]

As we continue to look at the narrative of unidentified phenomena and aliens, the proper description would be an alien is an extraterrestrial not of the Earth, or interdimensional but from a different dimension or other world; they are sentient beings. The Bible is very clear that sentient beings (aliens) chose to leave their habitation and live on the Earth with God's creation: "And the angels who did not keep their positions of authority but abandoned their proper dwelling—these he has kept in darkness bound with everlasting chains for judgment of the great day" (Jude 1:6).

There is another passage in the Bible that we have been using as a foundational scripture concerning alien life visiting mankind and using them to create a hybrid species: "And it came to pass when men began to multiply on the face of the earth, and daughters were born unto them, That the sons of God saw the daughters of men that they were fair; and they took them wives of all which they chose" (Genesis 6:1-2 KJV).

The nature of these sentient beings from the beginning of time has always appeared to humans in human form. They appeared in Sodom and Gomorrah, at the Resurrection, and the Ascension; they spoke and took men by the hand and ate meals; they appeared at Passover in Egypt and slaughtered 185,000 Syrians: "And it came to pass on a certain night that the angel of the Lord went out, and killed in the camp of the Assyrians one hundred and eighty-five thousand; and when people arose early in the morning, there were the corpses—all dead" (2 Kings 19:35 NKJV).

Nephilim/Watchers and alien technology have been around before the foundations of this earth. God, the Supreme Being (the Supreme Elohim), gave us a glimpse of ancient alien technology in the book of Ezekiel.

"This was the appearance and structure of the wheels: They sparkled like topaz, and all four looked alike. Each appeared to be made like a wheel intersecting a wheel. As they moved, they would go in any one of the four directions the creatures faced; the wheels did not change direction as the creatures went. Their rims were high and awesome, and all four rims were full of eyes all around.

When the living creatures moved, the wheels beside them moved; and when the living creatures rose from the ground, the wheels also rose. Wherever the spirit would go, they would go, and the wheels would rise along with them because the spirit of the living creatures was in the wheels. When the creatures moved, they also moved; when the creatures stood still, they also stood still; and when the creatures rose from the ground, the wheels rose along with them, because the spirit of the living creatures was in the wheels" (Ezekiel 1:16-21).

"As I looked, thrones were placed, and the Ancient of Days took his seat; his clothing was white as snow, and the hair if his head like pure wool; his throne was fiery flames; its wheels were burning fire. A stream of fire issued and came out from before him; a thousand thousands served him, and ten thousand times ten thousand stood before him; the court sat in judgment and the books were opened" (Daniel 7:9-19). Daniel in his dream was experiencing a vision and was transported to the courtroom of heaven before the throne of God, and was able to give us a graphic depiction of what he encountered.

The landscape of Daniel's dream, in its most fundamental aspect, mirrors Ezekiel's vision; it presents a Biblical narrative of the wheels burning in fire, the stream of fire that comes out before him, or his throne. The scripture's language portrays a majestic being on the throne and wheels burning in fire. Chariots are clouds, and these clouds represent angels; winds and clouds represent and are connected to angels.

In light of the Scriptures, this narrative concerning the living creatures are cherubims—the commanders of the living host—and the ones navigating this chariot or alien ship with wheels burning in fire are the commanders of the Lord: "The Lord reigneth; let the people tremble: he sitteth between the cherubims; let the earth be moved. The Lord is great in Zion; and he is high above all the people" (Psalms 99:1-2 KJV).

In Ezekiel 1:10, four creatures sit at the four corners of the earth and manage or supervise the affairs of the earth. The symbolism is that they are supervising the totality of what's going on with God's people. The number four represents universality; the Temple of Solomon had four cherubims/ sentient beings. Like the throne room of God, nothing in the universe escapes their attention.

"And after these things I saw four angels standing on the four corners of the Earth, holding the four winds of the Earth, that the wind should not blow on the Earth, nor on the sea, or on any tree. And I saw another angel ascending from the east, having the seal of the living God; and he cried with a loud voice to the four angels, to whom it was given to hurt the Earth and the sea, Saying, Hurt not the Earth, neither the sea, not the tree, till we have sealed the servants of our God in their foreheads" (Revelation 7:1-3 KJV).

God controls the whole narrative on Earth through these four angels, creatures, aliens, or sentient beings, and they are in control of all of the human events, holding back the passion of the seed of the serpent, who embodied the spirit of a genetic modification of the Nephilim.

"I watched till thrones were put in place, And the Ancient of Days was seated; His garment was white as snow, And the hair of His head was like pure wool. His throne was a fiery flame, its wheel a burning fire; A fiery stream issued, And came forth from before Him. A thousand thousands ministered to Him; Ten thousand times ten thousand stood before Him. The court was seated, And the books were opened" (Daniel 7:9-10 NKJV).

The four living creatures are in the process of moving the wheels of God's chariot, or spacecraft; the wheels that are at the right angle in the chariot of God, of God's throne, and can move at any direction at the speed of lightning (Ezekiel 10:15,16).

"The wheels were so complicated in arrangement that, at first sight, they appeared to be in confusion; but they moved in perfect harmony. Heavenly beings, sustained and guided by the hand beneath the cherubim's wings, were impelling these wheels; above them, upon the sapphire throne, was the Eternal One; round about the throne was a rainbow, the emblem of divine mercy." [9]

As the wheel-like complications were under the guidance of the cherubim's wings, the complicated plays of human events are under divine control. Some scholars and theologians believe the wheels represent the wheels of human history and the events that transpire on Earth. Could it also be some alien technology designed by the Supreme Elohim?

"Behold, there appeared a chariot of fire, and horses of fire, and parted them both asunder; and Elijah went up by a whirlwind into heaven, And Elisha saw it, and cried My Father, my Father, the chariot of Israel, and the horsemen thereof. And he saw him no more; and he took hold of his own clothes, and rent them in two pieces" (2 Kings 2:11-12 ASV).

Within the ethics of most Christianity, and our morals as Christians, the present worldview concerning alien technology and the Supreme Elohim is unnatural in the evolutionary narrative of the human race. As human beings, we must understand where we stand in the spectrum of creation and that man was not the first sentient being created; there were other realms, heavens, creatures, angels, and sentient beings that existed long before man was created on Earth.

Elijah being transported in a "chariot of fire," or an alien spaceship, or "the chariot of Israel" is not your normal chariot during this period. The Bible tells us that this chariot traveled vertically into the skies and had lights or fire as it took Elijah in a whirlwind into heaven.

In the paradigm of the period when Elijah was no more, we know the human race had not yet developed the technology of a flying object that could transport humans into the heavens. Still, we know that the Supreme

Elohim and the angels knew advanced technology: "For by Him (Christ) were all things created, that are in heaven, and that are in earth, visible and invisible, weather they be thrones, or dominions, or principalities, or powers: all things were created by Him and for Him And he is before all things, and by him all things hold together" (Colossians 1: 16-17 KJV).

This event has forever been written and recorded in the Bible and was witnessed by Elisha, even if it doesn't agree with your current theology or worldview. With all the reports and UFO sightings in recent years, we can't deny aliens or angels are visiting the human race; these encounters will be used for the Great Deception in the end times. From the beginning of time, Satan has always corrupted what God has created, which is why I believe the Bible is very adamant about a fifth angelic invasion.

"And war broke out in heaven; Michael and his angels fought with the dragon; and the dragon and his angels fought, but they did not prevail, nor was a place found for them in heaven any longer. So the great dragon was cast out, that serpent of old, called the Devil and Satan, who deceives the whole world; he was cast to the Earth, and his angels with him" (Revelation 12:7-12 KJV) an end-time angelic invasion.

16

THE BEAST

"Then another angel, a third one, followed them, saying with a loud voice, 'If anyone worships the Beast and his image, and receives a mark on his forehead or on his hand, he also will drink of the wine of the wrath of God, which is mixed in full strength in the cup of His anger; and he will be tormented with fire and brimstone in the presence of the holy angels and in the presence of the Lamb. And the smoke of their torment goes up forever and ever; they have no rest day and night, those who worship the Beast and his image, and whoever receives the mark of his name'" (Revelation 14:9-11 NASB).

The end time landscape, the empire of the son of perdition and the systems of his government, the kingdoms of this earth, the hierarchy families and secret societies, the royal families, and the ruling class of this present-day rebellion have allied with the unholy trinity: Satan, the Antichrist, the false prophets, and false teachers.

The one percent of the human race has established an alliance with the unholy trinity that rules the affairs of the earth. These are the earth's elite and influential families and secret societies: the Cult, the World Economic Forum, the Jesuit, the Club of Rome, the Club of 300, the Rothschilds, the Cabal, the Bilderberg Group, The Brotherhood of the Snake, the Druids, the Trilateral Commission, and the Bohemian Club to name a few.

The foot soldiers for these influential families and secret societies are the Freemasonry, the Illuminati, the Counsel of Twelve, the Knights of Columbus, the Knights Templars, the Ancient Babylonian Mystery Religion and the Catholic Church, The Women That Ride the Beast Nimrod, and the Skulls and Bones Society. These are the gateways and alliances for these elite families as we advance to the culmination of the end time to create a "New World Order," or "the World Economic Forum."

Who are they? "Morpheus, from The Matrix, quotes," "The matrix is a system Neo, that system is our enemy. But when you're inside you look around, what do you see? Businessmen, teachers, lawyers, carpenters. The very minds of the people we are trying to save. But until we do, these people are still part of that system, and that makes them our enemy. You have to understand most of these people are not ready to be unplugged. And many of them are so inured, so helplessly dependent on the system, that they will fight to protect it." [1]

As God's creation, we are all somewhat conscious of the world we live in, but have you been awakened?

These people have established an alliance with an Antichrist system in our society through money, politics, government, sex, LGBTQ, BLM, and "the World Economic Forum." You may think that you're awake, but the real question is, have you been awakened? What do I mean by awakened? As we are all being exposed to the system of our enemy, are you increasing in the knowledge of the Word of God concerning your personal journey from the beginning of time, "creation," the present world, "the system of the Kingdom," and what is to come, the end time church?

We all live in a simulation that God created, "the Matrix," composed of different dimensions or frequencies. We live in the third dimension within this simulation, the human world. In ancient cultures, the arena of the spiritual realm was called astral; in modern times, it's called the fourth dimension.

The fourth dimension is obtained through the subconscious and conscious mind harmonizing. One can experience a spiritual awakening and is no longer connected to the third dimension. This is what a person does to astral project—they project their non-physical body from their physical body, or what some call the "opening of the third eye."

The fifth dimension is a place of spirits of other beings that exist in the universe. It is where knowledge and awareness happen, or a revelation of who or what is controlling the fourth dimension. This is the spiritual realm of the demonic forces and demonic consciousness that is projected and manipulated through the second heaven. So these cults that I'm exposing are the very ones behind world events and what has been unfolding in recent years—an extension of an Antichrist system to create a "One World Government" or "The World Economic Forum." [2]

This is all demonic, and a true prophet of God will not function in this realm because this is not prophetic but witchcraft and divination.

A New World Order is a system without borders that will end the existence of the independent state; there will be an end to market economies but will be a centralized Socialist government, the World Economic Forum with a Centralized Banking System, and Central Bank Digital Currencies (CBDC).

The Biblical narrative of the Antichrist's origin is that he will be born of Jewish descent and from the tribe of Dan, as many theologians, historians, and early expounders have expressed. Still, today many expounders admit that this view lacks Biblical support.

"During the late-medieval period, we see a transition from a personal Antichrist to a corporate one as some Catholics and most Reformers tended to see the successive Popes and the Roman Church as Antichrist. However, the early and medieval church always saw an individual Antichrist.

For the last two hundred years, with the revival of the literal and thus futurist interpretation of prophecy, the historic Protestant notion that the

Antichrist was the system of the Roman Catholic Church has been in decline. Bernard McGinn tell us:

"After Vatican II, traditional Lutheran and Reformed claims that the Pope was Antichrist have been either forgotten or explicitly rejected. Even the Evangelical Fundamentalists, for whom Antichrist is alive and well, have been uncomfortable with a papal Antichrist." Regarding the tradition of a Jewish Antichrist, some of the earliest expounders of Antichrist, Irenaeus and Hippolytus of the second century, taught that Antichrist would be a Jew. McGinn says Irenaeus "depended on earlier traditions, both Jewish and Christian, in claiming that Antichrist would be born a Jew, specifically for the tribe of Dan." Hippolytus, a disciple of Irenaeus, wrote extensively on the Antichrist. Hippolytus believed that the "Antichrist is a Jewish false messiah whose coming is still some time in the future." Origen, Chrysostom, Jerome, and likely Augustine all continued the early church tradition that the Antichrist was to be of Jewish descent who would likely be of the tribe of Dan was reinforced throughout the Middle Ages. [3]

The coming world leader, "the Antichrist," is also presented in the book of Revelation. Who gives their power and authority to the Beast, who also receives his powers from Satan? The book of Daniel states that they shall mingle themselves with the seed of man again; in the last days, we will once again have hybrids walking the earth, half angel and half human, "the Beast."

"And the fourth kingdom shall be as strong as iron, inasmuch as iron breaks in pieces and shatters everything; and like iron that crushes, that kingdom will break in pieces and crush all the others. Whereas you saw the feet and toes, partly of potter's clay and partly of iron, the kingdom shall be divided; yet the strength of the iron shall be in it, just as you saw the iron mixed with the ceramic clay. And as the toes of the feet were partly of iron and partly of clay, so the kingdom shall be partly strong and partly fragile. As you saw iron mixed with the ceramic clay, they will mingle with the seed of men; but they will not adhere to one another, just as iron does not mix with clay"

(Daniel 2:40-43 NKJV). Daniel is interpreting the Nebuchadnezzar dream about a mixture of clay and iron which in the natural world was describing the final stage of the fourth kingdom which represents the Roman Empire. But prophetically I believe Daniels interpretation has a double meaning as Daniel's vision also gives a narrative presented in the book of Genesis of "the sons of God" having sexual relationships with "the daughters of man" and creating a hybrid species, half human and half angelic, a mixture of two different elements as in Genesis 6:1-4.

The word transplanted means "mingle or mix," the clay represents "the seed of the woman," and the iron represents "they, angels, the seed of the serpent," or the seed of Satan, or modern technology "as in the days of Noah."

"He will attack the mightiest fortresses with the help of a foreign god and will greatly honor those who acknowledge him. He will make them rulers over many people and will distribute the land at a price" (Daniel 11:39 NIV).

By changing the narrative at the beginning of creation, when "the sons of God came to the daughters of man," you can determine the narrative of the end times; these angels that did not keep their first estate have a dual meaning. First, they left their place of habitation, and second, they did not keep their heavenly bodies but took on the physical appearance of a human body.

The technology gained through the angels was dispersed in the Tower of Babel and kept through secret societies. Like in the days of Noah, it is coming full circle in this present age: "He will make them rulers over many people and will distribute the land at a price" (Daniel 11:39 NIV). This will be done through transhumanism, hybrids, super soldiers, cybernetics, nanotechnology, Neuralink, and the one percent of the human race that has already established an alliance with the unholy trinity that rules the affairs of the earth.

The book of 2 Thessalonians recounts a fascinating narrative of the Antichrist not fully human coming with aliens, "extraterrestrials" in the sky, an alien invasion, and an intriguing event, much like the Watchers in the Book of Enoch: "Concerning the coming of our Lord Jesus Christ and our being gathered to him, we ask you, brothers and sisters, not to become easily unsettled by the teaching allegedly from us-whether by a prophecy or by word of mouth or by letter asserting that the day of the Lord has already come. Don't let anyone deceive you in any way, for that day will not come until the rebellion occurs and the man of lawlessness is revealed, the man doomed to destruction. He will oppose and will exalt himself over everything that is called God or worshipped, so that he sets himself up in God's temple, proclaiming himself to be God" (2 Thessalonians 2:1-4 NIV).

With all of the propaganda and misfortune of 2020 in recent years concerning our government, the governments of the world, and China, the coverage of COVID-19 and how this incident accelerated the global Antichrist narrative is the method by which the Antichrist will perform and accomplish the overthrowing of world governments and systems is infiltrating the current global economic system and its attempt to collapse the international market.

The kingdoms of this earth, the hierarchy families, secret societies, royal families, and the ruling class of this present-day rebellion have allied with the unholy trinity: Satan, the Antichrist, and the false prophets. The commencement of a "Global Reset" has begun to create a "Global Digital Currency" through the "World Economic Forum."

"These are grumblers, complainers, walking according to their own lusts; and they mouth great swelling words, flattering people to gain advantage" (Jude 1:16 KJV).

The United States has been one of the greatest influencers in this narrative of the hierarchy of families and government in creating a "One

World Government" system, along with China and the European Union, by technology and artificial intelligence

"Technological leadership will require big digital investments, rapid business process innovation, and efficient tax and transfer systems." [4]

These events that have transpired in recent years are prophetic concerning the prophecy of the "Beast." These end time events will usher in a new world system, "the World Economic Forum," that will create the platform for the Antichrist to take his place as the authority of a new global system, a New World Order, and a One World Government.

In the book of John, the Apostle John describes the end times, the present generation, and the generations to come concerning the narrative of the Antichrist: "Little children, it is the last hour; and as you have heard that the Antichrist is coming, even now many antichrists have come, by which we know that it is the last hour" (1 John 2:18 NKJV).

The COVID-19 pandemic ushered us into the dispensation of end-time events and what is inevitably to come: the destruction of this present world, but not until all that has been prophesied is fulfilled.

The Four Horsemen of the Apocalypse is a narrative concerning some of the global end time events that will transpire during a time when the earth's inhabitants will experience unusual phenomena, including plagues, pandemics, pestilences, war conflicts, famines, food shortages, and strife.

I believe in the year 2020, according to the times and seasons and the chronological events in the Bible, that the first seal was opened and the first Horseman of the Apocalypse appeared, as prophesied in the book of Revelation: "The Lamb of God, the Lion of Judah opened the first seal"(Revelation 6:1 KJV).

"And I saw, and behold a white horse; and he that sat on him had a bow; and a crown was given unto him; and he went forth conquering and to conquer" (Revelation 6:2 KJV). The book of Revelation, apocalyptic and metaphorical in nature, speaks of the first seal being opened and a rider on a white horse to spread pestilence that he might conquer in the last days.

What will a Global Central Bank achieve by accepting BTC as a legal tender? The global economic banking system will rely on effective monetary policies, manage their economies, and will have the ability to implement their policies around the current economic threat to a banking system around the currency in times of a global economic collapse.

"The rise of Bitcoin (digital currency) and a few other decentralized cryptocurrencies has also catalyzed several central banks to consider digital currencies a more robust alternative to flat currencies. As a result, many countries, including China, the United Kingdom, the U.S., and India, are all working on their Central Bank Digital Currencies (CBCD)."[5]

In the chronicles of a globally centralized banking system, two countries have adopted cryptocurrency (BTC) as their legal tender. El Salvador is the first country to adopt cryptocurrency (BTC) as a legal tender. The second country to adopt electronic currency as a legal tender is the Central African Republic (CAR). They are embracing this new banking system that will be the gateway for a "New World Government" that will implement the scenario for the Antichrist to achieve global supremacy by controlling the global economic platform.

And most recently, the BRICS Alliance is working to create its own currency, says a Russian official. The bloc grouping of emerging economic heavyweights Brazil, Russia, India, China, and South Africa are reportedly working on their own currency—established on a strategy that does not defend the dollar or duro,"[6] In the evolution of our current global economic platform, as Americans, we must understand our economic platform and our role in a centralized banking system.

Our current narrative of the central banking system in the United States, "the Federal Reserve," was founded in 1913 to stabilize the American banking system. "This central banking system has three important features;

a central governing board—the Federal Reserve Board of Governors,—a decentralized operating structure of 12 Federal Banks, and a blend of public and private characteristics."[7]

Understanding the geographic landscapes of the Federal Reserve and how it operates very similar to private corporations, the question as Americans is, as the world prepares for a globally centralized banking system, is the Federal Reserve a government agency or a corporation governed by its board of directors?[8]

Chart 1 reveals the linear connection between the Rothschilds, the Bank of England, and the London banking houses, which ultimately control the Federal Reserve Banks through their stockholdings of bank stock and their subsidiary firms in New York.

The two principal Rothschild representatives in New York, J. P. Morgan Co., and Kuhn, Loeb & Co. were the firms that set up the Jekyll Island Conference at which the Federal Reserve Act was drafted. Who directed the subsequent successful campaign to enact the plan into law by Congress, and who purchased the controlling amounts of stock in the Federal Reserve Bank of New York in 1914?

"These firms had their principal officers appointed to the Federal Reserve Board of Governors and the Federal Advisory Council in 1914. In 1914 a few families (blood or business-related) owning controlling stock in existing banks (such as in New York City) caused those banks to purchase controlling shares in the Federal Reserve regional banks. Examination of the charts and text in the House Banking Committee Staff Report of August 1976 and the current stockholder's list of the 12 regional Federal Reserve Banks show this same family control."[9]

See the chart on the following page.[10]

The one percent of the human race has established an alliance with the unholy trinity which rules the affairs of the world and includes the likes of the Rothschilds, London, and the Bank of England—all majority

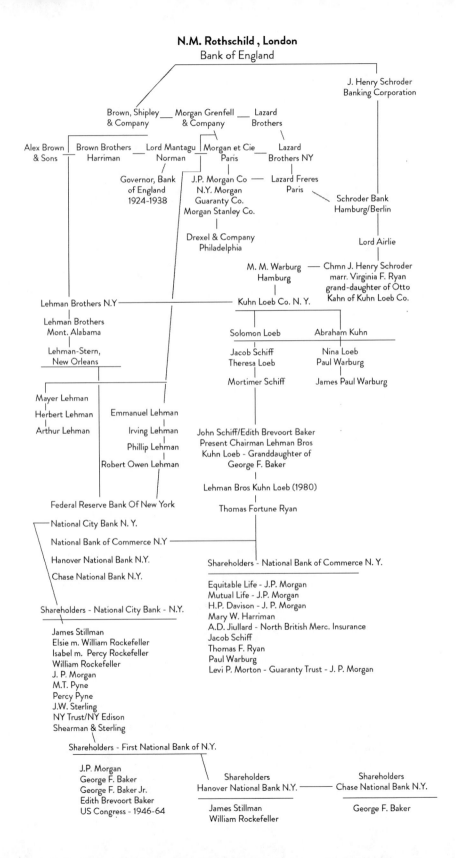

N.M. Rothschild , London
Bank of England

J. Henry Schroder
Banking Corporation

Brown, Shipley — Morgan Grenfell — Lazard
& Company   & Company   Brothers

Alex Brown | Brown Brothers   Lord Mantagu | Morgan et Cie   Lazard
& Sons | Harriman   Norman | Paris   Brothers NY

Governor, Bank   J.P. Morgan Co — Lazard Freres
of England 1924-1938 N.Y. Morgan   Paris
                      Guaranty Co.
                      Morgan Stanley Co.   Schroder Bank
                                               Hamburg/Berlin

                      Drexel & Company
                      Philadelphia   Lord Airlie

                              M. M. Warburg — Chmn J. Henry Schroder
                              Hamburg   marr. Virginia F. Ryan
                                             grand-daughter of Otto
                              Kuhn Loeb Co. N. Y.   Kahn of Kuhn Loeb Co.

Lehman Brothers N.Y

Lehman Brothers   Solomon Loeb   Abraham Kuhn
Mont. Alabama
                          Jacob Schiff   Nina Loeb
Lehman-Stern,   Theresa Loeb   Paul Warburg
New Orleans
                          Mortimer Schiff   James Paul Warburg

Mayer Lehman
                    Emmanuel Lehman
Herbert Lehman
                    Irving Lehman   John Schiff/Edith Brevoort Baker
Arthur Lehman   Present Chairman Lehman Bros
                    Phillip Lehman   Kuhn Loeb - Granddaughter of
                                     George F. Baker
                    Robert Owen Lehman
                                     Lehman Bros Kuhn Loeb (1980)

        Federal Reserve Bank Of New York
                                     Thomas Fortune Ryan

— National City Bank N. Y.

— National Bank of Commerce N.Y

Hanover National Bank N.Y.

Chase National Bank N.Y.   Shareholders - National Bank of Commerce N. Y.

                                  Equitable Life - J.P. Morgan
                                  Mutual Life - J.P. Morgan
                                  H.P. Davison - J. P. Morgan
Shareholders - National City Bank - N.Y.   Mary W. Harriman
                                  A.D. Jiullard - North British Merc. Insurance
                                  Jacob Schiff
James Stillman   Thomas F. Ryan
Elsie m. William Rockefeller   Paul Warburg
Isabel m. Percy Rockefeller   Levi P. Morton - Guaranty Trust - J. P. Morgan
William Rockefeller
J. P. Morgan
M.T. Pyne
Percy Pyne
J.W. Sterling
NY Trust/NY Edison
Shearman & Sterling

        Shareholders - First National Bank of N.Y.

        J.P. Morgan
        George F. Baker   Shareholders   Shareholders
        George F. Baker Jr.   Hanover National Bank N.Y. — Chase National Bank N.Y.
        Edith Brevoort Baker
        US Congress - 1946-64   James Stillman   George F. Baker
                                William Rockefeller

shareholders of the Federal Reserve. The global banking system is setting the stage for scripture to prophetically fulfill end time prophecy. We are in the times and seasons of the unveiling of the "Beast," and the Antichrist, the Son of the Dragon.

Now concerning the coming of this world leader, "the Antichrist," he will be born of a woman and fathered by Satan himself; he will be half human and half angel.

The narrative of Christ is that He was born of a virgin through conception by the Holy Spirit, so that means a conception by Satan will conceive the Antichrist.

God has Jesus as His Son, and Satan will have the Antichrist as his son. The Antichrist is a creative being in open opposition with God and His eternal divine purpose; he will be an outright enemy of God and the people of God in the last days.

"Who is the liar but the one who denies that Jesus is the Christ? This is the Antichrist, the one who denies the father and the son" (1 John 2:22 RSV).

It is important to recognize that "the Beast" is symbolic in nature of the Antichrist; the Beast is made in the likeness of the dragon, "Satan;" he is his biological son.

"And the beast which I saw was like unto a leopard, and his feet were as the feet of a bear, and his mouth as the mouth of a lion; and the dragon gave him his power, and his seat, and great authority" (Revelation 13:2 KJV).

As the coming of the end times approaches, there shall be significant events that will happen throughout the whole earth: "the outpouring of His spirit on all flesh; and many sons and daughter will be prophesying, and men shall be dreaming dreams, and young men shall see visions" (Joel 2:28).

The end time narrative of prophets and teachers prophesying and dreaming dreams also comes with a warning: beware of false prophets and false teachers. "And many false prophets shall rise, and shall deceive many" (Matthew 24:11 KJV).

Terullian (c 160–220 AD), held that the Roman Empire and the disintegration of the ten provinces of the Roman Empire into the ten kingdoms were to make way for the Antichrist: "For that day will not come unless the rebellion comes first," he (Paul) means this present empire indeed, "and the man of lawlessness revealed"—that is to say, the Antichrists. "The son of destruction, who opposes and exalts himself above every so-called God or rebellion, so that he takes his seat in the temple of God, is declaring himself to be God. Do you not remember that I told you these things when I was still with you? And you know what now is restraining him so that he may be revealed when his time comes. For the mystery of lawlessness is already at work, but only until the one who now restrains; is removed. What obstacles are there but the Roman state? The rebellion of which, scattered into the kingdoms, will introduce the Antichrist upon its ruins? And then the lawless one will be revealed, whom the Lord will destroy with the breath of his mouth, annihilating him by the manifestation of his coming. The coming of the lawless one is apparent in the working of Satan, who uses all power, signs, lying wonders, and every kind of wicked deception for those who are perishing." [11]

Most scholars agree that Rome will give birth to the last superpower before the coming of Christ. Rome will subdue the nations of the earth by influence and political, and spiritual power. It will be acquired through the Beast, the Antichrist, and the Son of the Dragon.

"So they worshipped the Dragon who gave authority to the Beast; and they worshiped the Beast, saying. Who is like the Beast? Who is able to make war with him? And he was given a mouth speaking great things and blasphemies, and he was given authority to continue for forty-two months. Then he opened his mouth in blasphemy against God, to blaspheme His name" (Revelation 13:4-6 NKJV).

The book of Daniel describes Daniel's vision concerning the Roman Empire as he predicts human-hybrids, iron mixed with ceramic clay, a mingling of seed of man and angels, and "the Ten Kings," which represent ten toes creating a hybrid species that will control the world's political system and global economic system.

"Whereas you saw the feet and toes, partly of potter's clay and partly of iron, the kingdom shall be devised; yet the strength of the iron shall be in it, just as you saw the iron mixed with ceramic clay. And as the toes of the feet were partly of iron and partly of clay, so the kingdom shall be partly fragile.

As you saw iron mixed with ceramic clay, they will mingle with the seed of men; but they will not adhere to one another, just as iron does not mix with clay. And in the days of these kings the God of heaven will set up a kingdom which shall never be destroyed; and the kingdom shall not be left to other people; it shall break in pieces and consume all these kingdoms, and it shall stand forever" (Daniel 2:41-44 NKJV).

The Book of Enoch and the Book of Genesis state that when the Watchers/fallen angels arrived on earth, they took wives, making a covenant with these women and their fathers in exchange for technology. In the last days, Iron will be mixed with ceramic clay again; Iron is those who possess advanced technology, which I believe are "angels," sharing technology with the human race, and ceramic clay is the human race, man. "And then the Lord God formed man of the dust of the ground, and he breathed into his nostrils the breath of life; and man became a living being" (Genesis 2:7 NKJV). The narrative of Genesis repeats itself—an angelic invasion, the return of the Nephilim, and "the Beast."

"As I watched, this horn, 'the Roman Empire' was waging war against the holy people and defeating them until the Ancient of Days came and pronounced judgment in favor of the holy people of the Most High, and the time came when they possessed the kingdom" (Daniel 7:21).

The time is coming when no man will be able to buy or sell without the mark of "the Beast."

"And he causeth all, both small and great, rich and poor, free and bond, to receive a mark in their right hand, or in their foreheads: And that no man might buy or sell, save he that had the mark, or the name of the beast, or the number of his name" (Revelation 13:16-17 ESV) the beast.

CONCLUSION

The first effort is to investigate and summarize God's unfolding theme in the Bible storyline. The theme is God's plan of creation over history and the origin of sin; from a creative perspective, we must understand the origin and composition of the Scriptures. In studying hermeneutics, we must accept that this view promotes that the Bible is one book and was given to us by one God.

"All scripture is given by inspiration of God, and is profitable, for doctorine, for reproof, for correction, for instruction in righteousness, that the man of God may be complete, thoroughly equipped for every good work" (2 Timothy 3:16-17 NKJV).

In studying hermeneutics, we accept the view of plenary and verbal inspiration. We believe in the plenary, verbal inspiration of the accepted canon of the Scriptures. As originally given, the Word of God is infallible, uniquely authoritative, and free from any kind of error in all matters that it deals with, including scientific, historical, moral, and theological issues.

As apostles, prophets, students, and teachers of the Scriptures, we must accept that all portions of the Bible are inspired and apply to the entire book. So we look at the word "plenary," which means "full or complete," so when we apply this to Scripture, it means God inspires the entire Bible. It's not based on a person's limited illumination and understanding of Scripture.

We must clearly understand the difference between revelation, illumination, inspiration, and application if we are doctrinally sound in the Scriptures.

"The secret things belong unto the Lord our God: but those things which are revealed belong unto us and to our children forever, that we may do all the words of this law" (Deuteronomy 29:29 NIV).

The Bible tells us of secret things that belong to Him and of things that He has revealed, but we also know that the Scriptures tell us that certain things have been hidden for a season. As we approach the end times, God is exposing the hidden truth of the Scriptures—illumination—and the divine ability to understand, that which is given by revelation.

"Concerning this salvation, the prophets, who spoke of the grace that was to come to you, searched intently and with the greatest care, trying to find out the time and circumstances to which the Spirit of Christ in them was pointing when he predicted the sufferings of the Messiah and the glories that would follow. It was revealed to them that they were not serving themselves but you, when they spoke of the things that had been told to you by those who have preached the gospel to you by the Holy Spirit sent from heaven. Even angels long to look into these things" (1 Peter 1:10-12 NIV).

As we look into the inspiration of Scripture, it is the ability to write down revelation without making a mistake; it is the process of recording the truth. This was the power that enabled the men of the Bible to write down things accurately.

"Inspiration is the strong conscious inbreathing of God into men, qualifying them to give utterance to the truth. It is God speaking through men, and the Old Testament is, therefore, just as much of the Word of God as though God spoke every single word of it with His lips. The Scriptures result from divine inbreathing just as human speech is uttered by breathing through a man's mouth." [1]

The Bible is a closed book for those who don't have an intimate relationship with God and are lost to the world. Still, the Bible is an open book to the believer who has separated himself, especially a Fivefold teacher with an Apostolic and Prophetic mandate. This message is clear throughout the Scriptures.

The Bible calls us to "Be diligent to present yourself approved to God, a worker that does not need to be ashamed and who correctly handles the word of truth" (2 Timothy 2:15). As we observed, the Bible is the story of God from the origin of sin, the destruction of the first earth and second earth, and the creation of the new earth, a new beginning for Noah and his family.

We also observed that the Kingdom of God is a physical reality that develops throughout redemptive history. Scripture reveals this Kingdom under the theme of God's people in His place under His rule. God designed the Scriptures to show His creation that He is a covenant-keeping God and has always planned to redeem a fallen creation.

We also saw that Satan, through the "sons of God," corrupted the genetic DNA of creation before and after the flood to destroy the bloodline of the Messiah. Still, in the end, God prevailed, and Christ was born to redeem a fallen creation back to its Creator.

I pray that as I expose Biblical truth, revelation, illumination, and inspiration of Scripture is imparted to those who read this book and that they will look at the evidence presented through Scripture as God continues to give us the illumination of His Word.

We are living in a time where the truth of the Gospel is not being preached from our churches. I truly believe there shall be a great falling away in the last days because the Church has been teaching a false gospel. In these end times, God is calling for a people that will rightly divide the word of truth without compromising for personal gain.

All history must be seen as the working out of God's eternal purpose that reflects God's glory and is to be pursued for His praise. This also includes a Christian philosophy of culture, which is art and science, and includes a Christian view of vocation: all callings are from God, and all we do in everyday life is to be done to God's praise. So let's honor God and bring glory to His name as students and teachers of truth in everything we do (1 Corinthians 10:31).

The Book of Enoch is mentioned in Jude and Peter. The Book of Jasher is mentioned in the Book of Joshua and Samuel. And the Book of Jubilees is not mentioned in the Bible by name. It is found in the Dead Sea Scrolls from about 1947-1956.

"The Greek translation to 1 Enoch was known to and referenced by many of the early church fathers, including Clement and Barnabas (the friends of Paul), Irenaeus, Origen, Tertullian, Athenagoras of Athens, and Justin Martyr, all of whom held an affirming view of the text." [2]

It is important to note that no modern scholar or theologian has ever asserted that the text presently called "The Book of Enoch" was actually written by the prophet Enoch. It is classified as pseudepigrapha - books that falsely use the name of a biblical figure to draw more attention and lend them an air of credibility they would not otherwise have. The earliest extant copy of the Book of Enoch is composed of six fragments found with the Dead Sea Scrolls, placing its origin at about 350-200 BC. A version of the Book of Enoch was in circulation in the first century AD as several church fathers disapproved of it. [3]

"There is no doubt that the Book of Enoch was accepted as at least informative (if not inspired) by some church members going back to the first century. However it was never considered a part of the Biblical canon by Jews of Christians in the first century AD." [4]

I pray that you have been blessed through my Apostolic and Prophetic writing, may God be glorified.

BIBLIOGRAPHY

Introduction

1. Reese, W. L. (1980). *Dictionary of Philosophy and Religion*, p 221). Sussex: Harvester Press.

Chapter 1

1. Ryrie, C. C. (1999). Basic Theology. *A popular systematic guide to understand biblical truth*, Moody Publishing.
2. Bonilla, D. (2018). *Journey through the Word*, Published by GPS Intense Internship, Journey Through The Word.
3. MacArthur, J. (2014). Scripture interprets Scripture") and are the final authority of Christian doctrine. *What does Sola Scriptura mean?* 2015, Wisconsin Evangelical Lutheran Synod. Archived from the Original in May 2014. Retrieved 22 May 2014).
4. The Editors of Publications International, Ltd. (2007, September 24). *9 types of Angels*. HowStuffWorks. https://people.howstuffworks.com/9-types-of-angels.htm

Chapter 2

1. Ball, S. (2003, September). *A Christian physicist examines the big bang theory*. https://www.letu.edu/academics/arts-and-sciences/files/big-bang.pdf
2. Swain, S. R. (2011b). Bibliography. *Trinity, revelation, and reading: A Theological introduction to the bible and its interpretation*. https://doi.org/10.5040/9780567660473.0007
3. Mathews, K. A. (1996). *Genesis. "Genesis 1-11:26,"* NAC, Vol. 1A Nashville: Broadman & Holman, 1996, 126-27).
4. Bonilla, D. (2018). *Journey through the Word*, Published by GPS Intense Internship, Journey Through The Word.

Chapter 3

1. Bonilla, D. (2018). *Journey through the Word*, Published by GPS Intense Internship, Journey Through The Word.
2. Bonilla, D. (2018). *Journey through the Word*, Published by GPS Intense Internship, Journey Through The Word.

3. VanGemeren, W. (2002). From Eden to Jerusalem: Town and country in the economy of redemption. *A theology of the built environment*, 114–137. https://doi.org/10.1017/cbo9780511487712.006

4. GPS Intensive Internship 2018, Danny Bomilla.

5. Bonilla, D. (2018). *Journey through the Word*, Published by GPS Intense Internship, Journey Through The Word.

6. Spencer, L. (2015, November 20). *Eschatology (last things)* – page 2. TheoThoughts. https://theothoughts.com/category/theology/eschatology-last-things/page/2

7. Baker, D. L., & Kelly's 4 Christ. (2014). *Two testaments, one Bible: The theological relationship between the Old and New Testament.*

8. Robinson, Robert Clifton. (2020). *There are actually 937 Scripture citations from the Old Testament that are found in the New Testament.* There Are Actually 937 Scripture Citations from the Old Testament That Are Found in the New Testament.

9. Bonilla, D. (2018). *Journey through the Word*, Published by GPS Intense Internship, Journey Through The Word.

10. Gemeren, V. (2024). *The progress of redemption: The story of salvation from creation to the New Jerusalem: Willem Vangemeren: 9780801020810: Amazon.com: Books.* Progress-Redemption-Salvation-Creation-Jerusalem; https://www.amazon.com/Progress-Redemption-Salvation-Creation-Jerusalem/dp/0801020816

11. Bonilla, D. (2018). *Journey through the Word*, Published by GPS Intense Internship, Journey Through The Word.

12. Bonilla, D. (2018). *Journey through the Word*, Published by GPS Intense Internship, Journey Through The Word.

13. Wahlberg, R. (2024). *251 biblical baby names.* BabyCenter. https://www.babycenter.com/baby-names/advice/baby-names-from-the-bible_10309862

14. Bonilla, D. (2018). *Journey through the Word*, Published by GPS Intense Internship, Journey Through The Word.

Chapter 4

1. Bonilla, D. (2018). *Journey through the Word*, Published by GPS Intense Internship, Journey Through The Word.

2. Copmton, A. R. (2018). *The Seed of The Women and The Seed of The Serpent at War:* The Seed of The Women and The Seed of The Serpent at War; https://knakkergaard.pro/musik/CrushedCats/EnclosuresDK/MigrationDK

3. Josephus, F. (2024, April 24). *Land of nod the Antiquities of the Jews (a. AD 93) that Cain was destined to live the life of an outsider, alienated from God and from His presence; he lost his identity and community.* Wikipedia. https://en.wikipedia.org/wiki/Land_of_Nod

4. Apud Euseb. Praepar. Evanel, (1903). *The Names given in This Verse of Scripture Tends to Focus on the Genealogy of Cain. "It Is Believed These Begat Sons, That Exceeded Others in Bulk and Height, Whose Names Were given to the Mountains They First Possessed, and from Them Were Called Cassius, Libanus, Antillibanus, and Brathy,"* 34–35.

5. Searchworld. (2019, April 21). *Cain's family tree.* (22) - Cain's Family Tree. Searchworld.org.uk.

6. Bonilla, D. (2018). *Journey through the Word*, Published by GPS Intense Internship, Journey Through The Word.
7. Bonilla, D. (2018). *Journey through the Word*, Published by GPS Intense Internship, Journey Through The Word.
8. Mathews, K. A. (1996). *Genesis. "Genesis 1-11:26,"* NAC, Vol. 1A Nashville: Broadman & Holman, 1996, 126-27).
9. Blender, B. (2011). *From Adam to Noah the genealogy of Adam* (Genesis 5:1-5:32). The Genealogy of Seth. Truthbookroom.com.sg

Chapter 5

1. Bonilla, D. (2018). *Journey through the Word*, Published by GPS Intense Internship, Journey Through The Word.
2. Author Chuck Missler. (1997). *Mischievous angels or sethites? Mischievous Angels or Sethites?* Koinonia House. https://www.khouse.org/articles/1997/110/

Chapter 6

1. Watch, F. (2023, February 3). *You won't believe what's in the Bible.* Not So Boring Bible. https://www.notsoboringbible.com/
2. Bonilla, D. (2018). Journey Through The Word, Published by GPS Intense Internship, Journey Through The Word.
3. Earthman, F. T. (2021, May 5). Things not taught in school and most churches. https://littleraventhepoet.blog/2021/05/14/things-not-taught-in-school-and-most-churches/

Chapter 7

1. Josephus, F. (2024, April 24). *Land of nod The Antiquities of the Jews (a. AD 93) that Cain was destined to live the life of an outsider, alienated from God and from His presence; he lost his identity and community.* Wikipedia. https://en.wikipedia.org/wiki/Land_of_Nod
2. Crispe, S. E. (2019). Spirituality & Feminine, Biblical Women: *"Chava: Mother of All Life."*
3. What is agriculture? - agrieco.net. What is Agriculture. (n.d.). https://agrieco.net/what-is-agriculture/
4. Walton, G. (2020). *Book of Ezekiel of the major prophetic books.* Book of Ezekiel of the major prophetic books; https://www.thebigwobble.org/2020/01

Chapter 8

1. Scott, L. (2024, May 8). *Botany. Wikipedia.* https://en.wikipedia.org/wiki/Botany
2. Christian, J. (2021). *Assessing the Impact of Heat Treatment on Antimicrobial Resistance genes and Their Potential Uptake by Other 'Live' Bacteria.* Wikipedia. https://doi.org/10.46756/sci.fsa.oxk34
3. Ott, U. F. (2016). *The DNA of Negotiations As a Set Theoretic Concept:A Theoretical and Empirical Analysis.* Wikipedia. https://doi.org/10.1016/j.jbusres.2016.01.007

4. MedlinePlus.gov. (2024). What is DNA? Medlineplus Genetics. MedlinePlus. https://medlineplus.gov/genetics/understanding/basics/dna/

5. Len.(n.d.).Biblical Health and Wellness.DNAintheBible. http://biblicalwellness.blogspot.com/

6. Len.(n.d.).Biblical Health and Wellness.DNAintheBible. http://biblicalwellness.blogspot.com/

7. Unknown. (2024). DNA in the Bible. http://gloryinthetruth.blogspot.com/2014/02/dna-in-bible.html?m=1

8. Len.(n.d.).Biblical Health and Wellness.DNAintheBible.

9. Len.(n.d.).Biblical Health and Wellness.DNAintheBible. http://biblicalwellness.blogspot.com/ biblicalwellness.blogspot.com/

10. HolyArt.com. (2023). Free will is the condition of thinking by virtue of which each of us (or angels) can determine the scope of their action with total autonomy. *Free Will Is the Condition of Thinking by Virtue of Which Each of Us (or Angels) Can Determine the Scope of Their Action with Total Autonomy.*

11. Harper, D. (2024). *Online etymology dictionary*. Etymonline. https://www.etymonline.com/

12. Foundation, W. (2024b, May 13)." *U*X*L encyclopedia of world mythology. . encyclopedia. com*. 15 Apr. 2024 .Encyclopedia.com. https://www.encyclopedia.com/literature-and-arts/classical-literature-mythology-and-folklore/folklore-and-mythology/satyr

13. Foundation, W. (2024a, March 24). *Sons of god*. Wikipedia. https://en.wikipedia.org/wiki/Sons_of_God

Chapter 9

1. Arendt, J. (2021, January 11). *The Supreme Court justices of roe vs. Wade: Mainly Republicans!*. James Japan. https://www.jamesjpn.net/government/the-supreme-court-justices-of-roe-vs-wade-mainly-republicans/

2. Nguyen, K. K. (2021). Center For Disease Control and Prevention. Abortion Surveillance-United States. https://www.cdc.gov/mmwr/preview/mmwrhtm1/

3. Blumberg, N. (2024, March 28). *The Bohemian Club*. Encyclopædia Britannica. https://www.britannica.com/topic/The-Bohemian-Club

4. Harbisson, N. (2024, May 8). *Transhumanism*. Wikipedia. https://en.wikipedia.org/wiki/Transhumanism

5. Researchers, U. of M. (2024). *Wary of human-animal hybrids? it's probably just your own moral superiority*. Find an Expert: The University of Melbourne. https://findanexpert.unimelb.edu.au/news/5943-wary-of-human-animal-hybrids%3F-it%27s-probably-just-your-own-moral-superiority.

6. Rigby, S. (2019). *Human-animal hybrids: Can we justify the experiments?* BBC Science Focus Magazine. https://www.sciencefocus.com/future-technology/human-animal-hybrids-can-we-justify-the-experiments

THE ORIGIN OF SIN

Chapter 10

1. Biblical Hermeneutics. (2023). Genesis-How did Nephilim reappear after the flood? Biblical Hermeneutics Stack Exchange. https://hermeneutics.stackexchange.com/
2. Biblical Hermeneutics. (2023). Genesis-How did Nephilim reappear after the flood? Biblical Hermeneutics Stack Exchange. https://hermeneutics.stackexchange.com/
3. Advacing Jewish Thought Mosaic. The Many Lives of Og the Giant King of Bashan, Hebrew Bible, Midrash Author Stuart Halpern, 2024 Mosaic, Design by MagCulture, Development by wire&Byte

Chapter 11

1. Tikkanen, A. (2024). *Deucalion*. Encyclopædia Britannica. https://www.britannica.com/topic/Deucalion
2. +Greekacom. (2024). *Myth of deucalion and pyrrha: Greeka*. Greekacom. https://www.greeka.com/sterea/delphi/myths/deucalion-pyrrha/
3. *(Herescope:TheResurrectionofPaganGodshttps:*. Herescope.blogspot.com. (2011). https://herescope.blogspot.com/2013/11/the-resurrection-of-pagan-gods.html
4. Laran, N. (2024, April 23). *Mars (mythology)*. Wikipedia. https://en.wikipedia.org/wiki/Mars_(mythology)
5. Wiki, C. to A. B. (2024a). Pluto. Astro Boy Wiki. https://astroboy.fandom.com/wiki/Pluto
6. Gods & Goddesses - A Guide to Mythological Deities. https://www.gods-and-goddesses.com/
7. Jupiter, W. (2023, November 23). *Jupiter (mythology)*. https://simple.wikipedia.org/wiki/Jupiter_(mythology)
8. O'Donoghue's, J. (2021). Neptune Facts. Neptune. https://space-facts.com-neptune/
9. Content Editors. (2024). Neptune: Facts - NASA science. NASA. https://solarsystem.nasa.gov/planets/neptune/in-depth/
10. The Planetary Society. (2024). pluto.dog-Pluto is a dwarf planet in the Kuiper Belt. pluto.dox-Pluto is a dwafplanetintheKulperbelt: https://www.coursehero.com/file/82264769/;plutododox/
11. Owen, T. C. (2024). *Charon*. Encyclopædia Britannica. https://www.britannica.com/place/Charon-astronomy
12. Dictionary.com. (2022, January 3). *Where does the name "January" come from?* https://www.dictionary.com/e/january/
13. Museum, B. (2017). *What's in a name? Months of the Year*. The British Museum. https://www.britishmuseum.org/blog/whats-name-months-year
14. Wikipedia Foundation Inc. (2024, April 22). How many days in April? https://en.wikipedia.org/wiki/April
15. Wikipedia Foundation Inc. (2024, April 30). AtlasWorldHistoryEncyclopedia. AtlasWorldHistoryEncyclopedia; https://worldhistory.org/Atlas/
16. janet.cameron104@facebook.com. (2024). *Is the month of June named after Roman goddess Juno?* Home page. https://decodedpast.com/is-the-month-of-june-named-after-roman-goddess-juno/

17. Trayteon, L. (2024). (LynTrayteonInstagram. July is the seventh month of the year. https://www.insta.com/p/CfeyeYCMc1-/
18. Cook, W. (1886). (*Explanations of Difficult Portions of Holy Scripture*).

Chapter 12

1. 69 Bible Verses about Nimrod, https://bibleportal.com/topic/nimrod
2. Isaiah Unfulfilled, Reverend Robert Govett, 1841.
3. Melissa Conrad Stöppler, M. (2023, November 30). 18 common genetic disorders: 4 types, symptoms, causes, human genome. MedicineNet. https://www.medicinenet.com/genetic_disease/article.htm
4. 5 Health Issues That areGeneticallyPassedDown,https://www.eatthis.com/news-health-issues-that-are-genetically-passed-down/
5. Truth Triumph: Or a Witness to the Two Witnesses, Thomas Tomkinson, 1690, a seventeenth-century theologian
6. Sodom and gomorrah israelahistoryof.com, https://www.israel-a-history-of.com/sodom-andgomorrah.html
7. Abraham, H. (1960). Asphalts and Allied Substances; Asphalts and Allied Substances; Volume One: Historical Review and Natural Raw Material.
8. Josephus, F., & Whiston, W. (1737). Antiquities of the Jews, Book 1, Chapter 4. University.
9. Roukema, R., & Deventer-Metz, S. (2010). Jesus, gnosis and dogma. T & T Clark.
10. Metaxas, E. (2017). Martin Luther; The Man Who Rediscovered God and Changed the World. Viking.
11. BBC World Services, Live Online UK Radio Stations; (1917). BBC World Services, Live Online UK Radio Stations. BBCWorld Services. http://uk-radio.com/bbc-world-services-1917
12. 1975-2022 Universal Co-Masonry. The American Federation of Human Rights, Inc. All Rights Reserved

Chapter 13

1. Johnson, W. (1908, April 23). *Megalith*. Wikipedia. https://en.wikipedia.org/wiki/Megalith
2. Hollingsworth, D. A. (1984). *Henry M. Morris and Creationism*. https://doi.org/10.2986/tren.001-1148
3. Banister, F. (2024, May 4). *Cyclopean masonry*. Wikipedia. https://en.wikipedia.org/wiki/Cyclopean_masonry
4. Steiner, M. L. (2022). Kathleen Kenyon and Jericho;
5. Willard, L. (2017). American Chemical Society National Historic Chemical Landmarks. *Discovery of Radiocarbon Dating*. Accessed October 31, 2017).
6. Mithen, S. (2006). *After the Ice: A Global Human History, 20,000-5000 BCE*. Harvard University Press.

7. Barton, G. A. (1973). Excavations at *jerichojericho, die ergebnisse der ausgrabungen*. Ernst Sellin , Carl Watzinger. *The American Journal of Semitic Languages and Literatures*, 30(4), 58. https://doi.org/10.1086/369751
8. The Reality of the Genesis 6 Giants: Prophecy Watchers; (2022). "The *Reality of the Genesis 6 Giants: Prophecy Watchers*."
9. Arnold, L. (2014). *In Music Theory & Education*.
10. Zola, A. (2022). *Tech Target*.

Chapter 14

1. Simpson, J. A., & C., W. E. S. (2001). The Oxford English dictionary. Clarendon Press.
2. Freedman, D. N., Myers, A. C., & Beck, A. B. (2000). Eerdmans Dictionary of the Bible. *Eerdmans Dictionary of the Bible, Wm. B Eerdmans Publishing: 2000, p 543*).
3. Hyman, S. (2022). (BT Satah Loc. Cit) (Meir, Tamar. "Orpah: Midash and Aggadah." *The Shalvi/Hyman Encyclopedia of Jewish Women. December 31, 1999. Jewish Women's Archive. Viewed on August 12, 2022*).
4. Jewish Women Archive. (1998). Encyclopedia of Jewish Women (Shalvi/ Hyman and December 31, 2009).

Chapter 15

1. Craine, A. G., & Collins, F. (2022). "Encyclopedia Britannica, Accessed August 17 2022). https://www.britannicaa.com/bigraphy/Francis-Collins.
2. Kurzwill, R. (2001). *"The Law of Accelerating Returns," Kurzweil Accelerating Intelligence*. http://www.kurzweilai.net/the law of accelerating-returns
3. Sentientmedia. (2024). *Stories + solutions for a changing world*. Sentient. https://sentientmedia.org/
4. Hamp, D. (2021). According to the Command of Great God Batios: *A New Translation of the Mt Hermon Stele Revealing Enlil's Logorgram, Corrupting the Image 2: Hybrids, Hades, and the Mt Hermon Connection.*
5. Parsons, H. (2024). *What's happened since CERN fired up the LHC again?* Gaia. https://www.gaia.com/article/whats-happened-since-cern-fired-up-the-lhc-again
6. Parsons, H. (2022). Seeking Truth, Secret & Cover Ups, Conspiracy; *Seeking Truth, Secret & Cover Ups, Conspiracy.*
7. Wikipedia The Free Encyclopedia. (2023, August 16). United Nations. Wikipedia. https://en.wikipedia.org/wiki/United_Nations
8. Yuhas, A. (2020). The Pentagon Released U.F.O. Videos: Updated September 1, 2021.
9. White, E. G. (2024). *Education*. Education, by Ellen G. White. Chapter 19: History and Prophecy. https://www.ellenwhite.info/books/bk-ed-19.htm

Chapter 16

1. Wachowski, L. (1999). *The Matrix, Laurence Fishburn as Morpheus.*
2. Fractal Enlightenment. (2026, March 30). Fractal enlightenment. Fractal Enlightenment ~ We Are All One. https://fractalenlightenment.com/

3.   McGinn, B., & Collins, H. (1994). *Antichrist: Two Thousand Years of The Human Fascination With Evil*, San Francisco: P. 59, 63, 252.

4.   Gill, I. (2020). *BROOKINGS, Future Development, Whoever Leads in Artificial Intelligence in 2030 Will Rule the World until 2100, Friday, January 17, 2020).*

5.   Cointelegraph 2013-2022

6.   Mitra, A. (2023). MINT, BRICS alliance working to create its own currency, says Russian official: MINT, BRICS Alliance, 02 Apr 2023. 10:25 PM IST (*Jagran Josh*, Arfa Javid, updated: Jun 21, 2023 12:22 IST).

7.   Board of Governor of the Federal Reserve System. (2024). Who owns the Federal Reserve? Board of Governors of the Federal Reserve System. https://www.federalreserve.gov/faqs/about_14986.htm

8.   Federal Reserve Directors: A Study of Corporate and Banking Influence Published 1976

9.   Krautkramer, W. N. (2024). The Federal Reserve - Its Origins, History Current Strategy. The Federal Reserve - its origins, History & Current Strategy. https://news.goldseek.com/GoldSeek/1095269452.php

10.   Baker, G. F. (1976). The Federal ReserveDirectors: A Study of Corporate and Banking Influence: Staff Report, Committee on Banking, Currency and Housing, House of Representatives, 94th Congress, 2nd Session.

11.   Wikipedia, the free encyclopedia. (2024b, May 9). *Antichrist*. Wikipedia. https://en.wikipedia.org/wiki/Antichrist

Conclusion

1.   Great Doctrines of the Bible; William Evans

2.   Internet Innovations, Inc. (2024). The book of enoch. The Book of Enoch and The Secrets of Enoch. https://reluctant-messenger.com/enoch.htm

3.   Pitterson, R. (2017). *Judgment of the Nephilim, Published by Days of Noe Publishing, New York: NY, Merrill, Eugene H., Everlasting Dominion: A Theology of the Old Testament, Nashville: B&H, 2006* . Days of Noe Publishing.

4.   Pitterson, R. (2017b). Judgment of the nephilim. Days of Noe Publishing.

ABOUT THE AUTHOR

Dr. Benjamin Martinez is the overseer of Benjamin Martinez Ministries, located in Jupiter, Florida. Gifted with a strong prophetic and teaching call, he has ministered in the United States, Puerto Rico, and overseas in Ecuador. He and his wife Josefina (Josie) Jalil Martinez served as part of the pastoral team of Hosanna Christian Fellowship in New York City for twenty-one years and then relocated to Jupiter, Florida; he now attends with his wife of forty-two years Power Of God Empowerment Ministries Inc., under the leadership of Apostle Ronnie Adderly and Prophet Robert Adderly.

Made in the USA
Columbia, SC
24 February 2025

14b5e811-fe21-403e-af7f-03b2e4110cafR01